Fisherman's Summer

RODERICK HAIG-BROWN

Fisherman's
Summer

Illustrated by Louis Darling

CROWN PUBLISHERS, INC., NEW YORK

Dedicated to the memory of Donald Arthur Lansdowne, age twelve, who was drowned when his canoe turned over at Siwash Rock in the Nimpkish River, 30 June 1957.

He knew the waters and loved them.

Library of Congress Cataloging in Publication Data

Haig-Brown, Roderick Langmere Haig, 1908-
    Fisherman's summer.

    1. Fishing.   I. Title.
[SH441.H142   1975]   799.1'2   74-32478
ISBN 0-517-51896-1

Preface to the 1975 Edition

I still think summer is the pleasantest time to go fishing —perhaps more than ever now that I am getting a little creaky in the joints and more sensitive to the chill of spring and winter.

If I were to write again of a fisherman's summer I should certainly write of Iceland, because I have found there in two recent years some of the finest fishing in one of the loveliest countries I have ever known. Whether it really qualifies as summer fishing I am not quite sure. There can be almost perfect days, cloudless and warm. There can be other days when an ice-cold wind comes down straight from the ice floes round the North Pole at twenty or thirty miles an hour and two layers of down clothing will not keep you warm. But summer fishing it is, July fishing, and if July weather in Iceland is somewhat variable, it is no more so than the July weather of the Canadian Arctic.

Everywhere in the temperate climates the precise timing of summer can be quite evasive. In this year of 1974, here on Vancouver Island, summer simply was not, until the last third of July. Then it became summer incomparable, gleaming day after gleaming day, and so persisted until the very end of September. This is roughly a month short of astronomical summer, which is reckoned from the summer solstice on June twenty-first to the autumnal equinox on September twenty-second or twenty-third. But it is far away from what the Oxford dictionary considers summer "in popular use" in the Northern Hemisphere: from mid-May to mid-August. I don't think I can recall a year when summer extended so plainly, without a break, all through September, as this year. I could not quite feel it to be summer, in spite of its perfection, because the salmon were swarming back into the river and that is fall to my river-oriented mind. Or were they perhaps just a little later this year, say a week or ten days slower to come in from salt water?

This is how a fisherman (or a farmer, for that matter) is about seasons. They never quite fit with his expectations, but it is always easy to explain why not. Of course the salmon were a little late this year. That high, hot sun made them reluctant to move into the shallow exposures of the rivers; and when they did come in, the big chinooks clung later and longer to the deep water of the canyon pool and the fast, deep flows elsewhere in the river. The first part of this is theory, but the second part is observation, matched against dated observations of other years.

The uncertainties of the seasons are a good part of their charm. They are a constant reminder that natural things are not grooved into rigid timetables and are not likely to be. A fisherman looks forward to the familiar things of his seasons; in summer the newly hatched merganser broods along the river, the return of the ospreys, the yellow warblers, and the swainson's thrushes, the chatter of kingfishers, the elegant flight of swallows, and the confiding presence of spotted sandpipers on familiar rocks and sandbars. He will expect the fritillaria lilies and tiger lilies and forget-me-nots to bloom along his riverbanks. He will watch for special fly hatches to repeat the patterns of other years. Often there is a surprising precision in these things, but all of us know the hazards of calling them too precisely. They will come in their time, very close to the time they always come, but not necessarily to the day. Many things can happen to change the day or even the week.

Part of the joy of fishing, of rivers, of their fish and all the life about them, will always be in their unpredictability. Part of it will always be in their predictability. What greater joy is there than going back to the same beloved place at the remembered time and finding that it has all kept faith; whatever made the magic a year ago or ten years ago is back in place precisely as it should be? Knowledge is vindicated, an intimacy somehow affirmed. Yet if it is different in some degree, if old knowledge is not confirmed but new knowledge is found, the rewards are just as great and intimacy is extended and enriched.

Fishermen are searchers. It is true we search for fish, at times with great diligence. But we search also, as men always have, for experiences; and there are no greater experiences than the seasons, varied and repeated year after year in our special comings and goings.

Roderick Haig-Brown
October, 1974

Contents

PART ONE

The Scene

1. *Summer Defined*

Bʏ ᴛʜᴇ ʙᴏᴏᴋs, sᴜᴍᴍᴇʀ sᴛᴀʀᴛs ɪɴ ᴍɪᴅ-June or a little beyond. Personally I am willing to call any warm and sunny day in June, or possibly even in May, a summer day, if only to flatter spring. And I am just as willing to talk about "spring run-off" when the snow melt comes pouring down the hills through late June and on into July. Seasons are quite flexible things really and it's not very profitable to try and tie them down to dates.

The end of summer comes where I live with the first rain and southeast gales of September—there is no doubt they do change things. Yet this year we are well into October and a week ago today I was sweating in waders and shirtsleeves as I worked up across the gravel bars of the Elk River, with the sun beating down into the narrow valley. I was glad to turn off into the dark cold of the canyon below Lady Falls on Cervus Creek, wading chest-deep in the 47-degree water until the chill got through to me—then I was glad to get back to gravel bars and sunlit water of the Elk. October it may have been, but summer it seemed and could well be counted.

Summer is not considered the best of times for the fresh-water fisherman. Trout lakes are generally too warm and the fish are deep and lazy. Streams are low and clear, the fish are likely to be shy and difficult. Here on the Pacific Coast the salmon are beginning to home and most fishermen turn to salt water, to troll or mooch for the big king salmon and the brilliant cohos. The trout lakes will be cooling off by mid-September, but not much before. The salt-water harvest goes on well into October and the streams are little used until the winter steelheaders come out to look for early runs towards the end of November.

I am willing to concede that the lakes may be off in the hot weather, and even that the abundance of salt water can have its attractions. But summer days are golden days and for me summer streams are golden streams. I love the freedom from bulky clothing, the feel of cool water against my waders, the thought of a bottle of beer or two cached some-where under the shade of the bank and the certainty that a few hours of wading and casting will arouse the thirst to do them justice.

Most of all I love the streams themselves at low water.

They are stripped of fat then, to bone and muscle. One can see the shape and interplay of the bones and watch the flow of sinew and muscle over and around them. Little runs and riffles that were hidden under the force of the snow run-off are suddenly clear and sparkling. Great rocks that scarcely creased the current surface now break it to white water or stand boldly out in the air from the pool bottom. Little glides that were lost and lapped in torrent flow are suddenly glides again to shelter a fish and welcome the kiss of a fly. The trees along the banks are heavy with green and hushed. It is a peaceful time for no one hunts and the ruffed grouse and the merganser broods are safe and undisturbed. The river warblers, yellow and Audubon, sit tight on their nests or feed their fledglings. Robins are busy with second broods and the hermit thrushes look over their nest rims with anxious eyes, but stay there crouched and still until the passerby is gone.

Along the streams, we fish: kingfisher, heron, merganser, water ouzel and I, with perhaps a sharp-eyed mink or a playful nuisance of an otter to make an occasional diversion. The sun lights the river clear to the pool bottoms and some-times shows up the shapes or casts the shadows of fish against them. The water feels and sounds different—it is kindly and welcoming, willing for once to commune its secrets. One moves slowly, carefully and attentively, for it is a good time to experiment and learn.

In summer the gravel bars are bare and travel is easy. One walks them in the hot sun and comes gladly to another crossing of the stream, to another bar and so to another pool. It is in summer that one finds, only half-believing, the big fish waiting in the little bubbling run near the head of the pool, drops the fly and sees every move from the first quiver of his fins as he lifts to it. In summer one searches the silent slicks that draw down, even faster, from the body of the pool. In summer the sedges hatch and the side creeks bring down the abundance of floating and drifting life that drops from the leaves of salmonberry, thimbleberry, huckleberry and snowberry lacing over them.

Summer is the time of little rods and light tackle, of the light foot and the careful approach. In summer the caddis larvae carpet the stream bottoms, the bears come down for the berries, the doe with her fawn and the cow elk with her calf wade the water at dusk. In summer the bandtailed pigeons talk and click their wings in the tall trees, the flycatchers hover and the swallows swoop and rise like dancers. In summer the evenings are long and the pool that was dead through the day comes suddenly alive.

Man was meant for summer, and summer for man—not summer of the desert and dusty sands, but summer with running water in the cool murmur of the hills. And what better excuse is there for being there than a fly rod in one's hand?

I first learned to fish in summer holidays from school and never gave thought to theories that it might not be a good time to fish. The stream was there, the fish were in it and fish in a stream were to be tempted, risen, hooked and landed. If they chose to lie on the bottom through the heat of the day, there would be a hatch later and they would come up. If they chose to be shy and difficult in the bright clear water, then it was a fisherman's part to stalk them, reach them and deceive them, himself undetected. And to this day I would rather see a fish, creep up to him and watch his rise to my fly than catch half-a-dozen fish unseen until they took.

I would not discount the other seasons. Each has its own values, sharp and positive and clear. But if fishing is the quiet sport of the contemplative man, then summer is the time of times for it, when the mind and body are relaxed and easy, the sun is warm and bright, the colors strong and the days long. A man should think when he is fishing, of all manner and shapes of things, flowing as easily through his mind as the light stream among its rocks. And the mind thinks best when the body is comfortable. All summer is not sunlight and the gray days and the stormy days may be the days when the fish rise best. But for me summer is low water and high sun, visible fish and difficult fish. And I know no lovelier time.

2. *Fisherman's Summer*

I SIT DOWN TO WRITE *Fisherman's Summer* in the early fall of 1958, seven or eight years after *Fisherman's Spring*, four or five years after *Fisherman's Winter*. I do so with a sharp sense of pleasure. For the past three years I have been immersed in the history of my province, fumbling my way through hours upon hours of research and writing slowly and painfully, on a desk piled high with references. It isn't that I haven't enjoyed it all, or failed to profit immensely by it—there are some delightful sidelights on fish and fishing in the early works of this part of the world—but it will be a pleasure now to write for a while off the top of my head, as a lightweight writer should.

There is a great deal to write about. Not that I myself have done such an enormous amount of fishing in the past four or five years, though I suppose I have done my share and I have certainly been lucky in some of my chances. But things have been happening fast in the world of fish and fishing—things that we all foresaw in outline twenty or thirty years ago, but could not judge in detail—and there is a good deal to be said about them. The stream bottoms today are paved with spinning lures and the rocks festooned with broken monofilament. It makes a difference in many ways. One can still get away to remote places, but most of us fish close in much of the time; there is a higher reward than ever before in knowing and understanding water, in the inspired guesses good fishermen make at the ways and fancies of the fish and in the thoroughness that makes chances count as they should.

While all this has been going on, the biologists have been learning more—and understanding less, I sometimes think— and often changing their views. Industry has been acting like a mad beaver, building dams in every direction, polluting watersheds, stealing parks and shutting away more and more land and good water to its own uses.

The ordinary, quiet, unassuming and vocationally gentle angler does not have to pay too much attention to all this, but I find it useful occasionally to examine it and assess it and see just what it does to me; and I think this is one of those times. I don't mean to beat up a mixture of the financial page, a biologist's pamphlet and a tourist guide. But I fancy a good part of my theme will be change and how best to operate within it and in spite of it.

Change is a worrying thing to all hunters and fishermen. So much of our skill depends on what we have learned of conditions and probabilities, often in the eager and vigorous days of youth, and it is not easy to start out to learn it all over again. Yet there can be a lot of fun in such learning; in fact it may be just what is needed to start a livelier interest and stir the fires of youth again. If so, it is a blessing and not a curse at all. My own home river, the Campbell, has been changed out of all knowledge. I resent the changes and certainly they have destroyed much that was precious. But since the sequence of changes has settled into something like recognizable stability, I find myself fishing harder than

for years past, with a curiosity as avid as that of my earliest
days and more exciting because, I flatter myself, better
informed.

From the declining years of the very first fisherman right
up to the present, I am reasonably sure that fishing never
has been what it was in the days of youth. But each new
generation has found its own days of youth, fished on
through maturity with considerable satisfaction, recognized
the decline of the erstwhile glories—and cheerfully gone on
fishing and complaining. I propose to follow on in the same
splendid tradition, because it is a very comfortable one and
somehow flattering to an ancient ego. But even in the depths
of my complaining I am fully aware that the sport will go
on, that new generations will enjoy it and that they will
find plenty to enjoy. I am convinced that there are a good
many reasons to believe that over the next fifty years fishing will actually become better than ever before, at least
along this Pacific slope of North America.

And I still believe that this is a good and important thing.
The more I see of men who go fishing and the satisfactions
they get from it, the more certain I am that the effort so
many good people have put into the development and preservation of the sport over the past four hundred and fifty
years has been thoroughly worthwhile. It worries me a little
to think that the sport has become, in North America, something of a social phenomenon, that learned theorists concern
themselves with such problems as the distribution of angling
pressure, the management of the angling public and other
matters that are sociological rather than sporting; but at the
same time I can't help recognizing this as one more tribute
to the enormous power and appeal of the sport. For the first

time in history a whole population has time and money and opportunity for extensive recreation; and men, women and children in overwhelming numbers have chosen to devote much of this precious time to probing the depths and the shallows, bright waters and dark, with humble fishing lines.

I do not want to manage or control anyone, or even to instruct. But I would claim again the privilege of sharing some fishing experiences and some thoughts about fishing with the many good anglers and good sportsmen who have been kind enough to enjoy what I have written before—and perhaps even a few who come upon this book entirely by chance. Fishing to me is not, as some of my critics have suggested, a way of life. But it is one of the keenest and best-wearing pleasures of life. There are deep and glowing things in even the simplest day on a river, and even more in the retrospect of such a day, which are worthy of honest examination.

PART TWO

How It Once Was

1. *The Explorers*

W<small>E ALL THINK SOMETIMES OF THE</small>
golden days in the land, when every stream ran unspoiled
to the sea, when the tall trees stood and the lakes were
untouched and fish were everywhere in unsophisticated
abundance. How would it have been to come, full-armed
with rods and reels and lines and flies, to such a land—
especially to this mountain land of British Columbia, with
lakes in every hollow and depression, rushing streams in
every valley and the best of fish in nearly all of them?

For a fairly sophisticated fisherman of today, it might
have been all right, in spots. He would have had his troubles

getting around, of course, and even greater troubles in de-
ciding just what he was looking for—the adjustment from
Atlantic salmon to steelhead, from eastern brook trout and
brown trout to rainbow and cutthroat is not the simplest
thing in the world, even when you know they are there.
Above all, he would have had his troubles with local knowledge. The Indians could have offered him some, if they
had understood his questions and if he had known how to
interpret their answers. But for the most part local knowledge of the type he really needed would have been impossible to find and time and again he would have passed up
just the right pool or just the right lake margin when he
was within a few hundred yards of it. In spite of this it
would have been a great adventure and no doubt he would
have happened on fabulous fishing time and again, to the
delight of himself and the often hungry natives. But the
opportunities he would have missed, in spite of all his so-
phistication, would certainly have turned his hair gray
could he have learned of them by some later revelation.

The truth is that it would have been a fairly difficult
business and an enormous amount of time would have been
wasted, pleasantly enough no doubt, in following up false
leads and mistaken hunches. And this may well have been
why the early explorers, among waters teeming with fish,
so rarely caught any—they had no time to check on leads
or follow hunches.

But at the same time the early explorers had the best of
all possible reasons to do something about the possibilities
of catching fish—they were often hungry and sometimes on
the verge of starvation. And they had ideal opportunities,
because they nearly always traveled by water, along the

rivers and lakes by canoe and along the intricate seacoast by sailing ships and small boats. Yet I cannot recall a single instance of a really successful fishing operation; instead they were content to struggle along on their own hard rations of pemmican or bully beef and biscuits, occasionally to barter for a few fresh fish from the natives or, often enough, simply to go hungry.

Captain George Vancouver and his men, who explored and charted the whole northwest coastline from California to Alaska through three long summers, were among the worst of the ineffectives, and it wasn't that they didn't have fishing gear aboard; Vancouver left a detailed account of the type and quality of stores and equipment sent out with his ships and carefully noted that: "in addition to the ordinary establishment, we were supplied with a large assortment of seines and other useful fishing gear of various kinds."

For three summers they were in the home waters of the greatest salmon runs in the world, with the fish feeding, migrating and showing all about them; they were over halibut banks and cod banks and among shoals of herring. And what came of it all? In Burrard Inlet the Indians "promised an abundant supply of fish the next day; our seine having been tried in their presence with very little success"; in Finlayson Channel: "this little bay is formed by a stony beach, through which a considerable run of water falls into the sea; this flattered us with the hope of taking a few fish, but the seine was worked to no other purpose than that of tearing it to pieces, nor were we more successful with our hooks and lines"; near Gardner's Canal things picked up a little: "the next morning the seine was

hauled and a good meal of fish procured for all hands."
Vancouver wasted no time in naming his anchorage Fisherman's Cove, "from our success in procuring fish, which in
these regions were a very scarce commodity." Yet in Gardner's Canal itself the small boats met with some natives who
"behaved in a very friendly and civil manner and presented
the party with two fine salmon, each weighing about
seventy pounds; these were the finest and largest that had
been seen during our voyage. . . ."

A great part of the exploration was done in small boats,
cutters and launches rowed by eight or ten men, which
worked out from the ships for two or three weeks and
sometimes longer and almost invariably ran out of provisions well before their return. No one seems to have
thought of trolling a hook and line, yet the most primitive
sorts of lures would certainly have picked up a few salmon
time and again and made an enormous difference not only
to comfort, but to health and efficiency.

One unhappy venture with fish—shellfish—brought about
one of the few deaths of the voyage. In Poison Cove at the
head of Mussel Inlet, off Milbanke Sound, Midshipman
Barrie and the crew of his small boat breakfasted on roasted
mussels, as they had often enough before. Very soon after
they "were seized with a numbness about their faces and
extremities; their whole bodies were very shortly affected
in the same manner, attended with sickness and giddiness."
Barrie ordered his men to row vigorously and took an oar
himself "in order to throw themselves into profuse per-
spiration," which helped a little for as long as they could
stand it. But in the end they had to put ashore and drink
warm water in the hope that "the offending matter might

have been removed"—all of them, that is, except poor John
Carter who was too far gone to swallow and died very
quietly about half an hour later. They buried him there,
a twenty-four-year-old Englishman from Mitcham in Sur-
rey. His grave is still to be found, marked by an outline of
rocks and a new headstone, and the place is called Carter
Bay.

A month or two later in the same year, on a small boat
trip of twenty-three days that explored Behm Canal in
the Alaska panhandle, Vancouver admits to having seen
great numbers of salmon "not only in all the arms, but in
almost every run of fresh water, particularly near the ter-
minations of the several inlets, where they were innumerable, though most of them were in a sickly condition."
Seines, hooks, lines were all forgotten. The men simply
waded into the streams and found no difficulty in taking
"as many of the best as we were inclined to make use
of. . . . They were all small, of one sort, and were called
by us hunch-backed salmon; from an excrescence that rose
along the upper part of the backs of the male fish."

This was around August 11 or 12 of 1793. The humpbacks were already spawning and mostly in very poor condition, but many of the fish in the inlets would have been
cohos and king salmon still in perfect condition. Almost
any piece of bright metal or even a white rag on a hook
would surely have taken a few of them and it is hard to
understand how it was that not one of the officers or sea-
men seems to have thought of trying such a thing. Some
of them must have had memories of trolling for mackerel
or sea bass in the North Sea or the English Channel.

Yet, when the ships put in at the Cocos Islands on the

way home in 1795, they had wonderful fishing. Vancouver
wrote, after a vivid description of the abundance and activity of sharks: "The other kinds of fishes that fell under
my notice . . . were two sorts of bream, a large snapper
of the West Indies, a sort of rockfish, and another kind
commonly called yellowtail; these were all very excellent
and took the hook readily." They were in warm tropical
seas then, and somewhat in holiday mood. There was time
and freedom to think about fish and how to catch them.
But one man with the fishing instinct, given a few days to
experiment in Puget Sound or the waters behind Vancouver
Island during the first summer of exploration, would have
learned enough to make the whole voyage much easier and
pleasanter. And among the hundred men of the *Discovery*
and the forty-five aboard the *Chatham* there must certainly
have been more than one man who would have had just
the touch to solve some of the problems of catching the
bright, fresh salmon that were jumping or finning or showing bubbles all around them. No doubt in his old age,
fishing for roach by Thames or Ouse, he thought back with
regret to the days of missed opportunity.

British Columbia's second explorer, Alexander Mackenzie, seems to have done no better. He worked his way up
the Parsnip, but no one thought to stop and make a catch
of whitefish and grayling. He came to the Fraser when it
was already full of salmon and still had only what fish the
Indians could provide. He and his party walked the West
Road River, short of provisions all the way, and left no
record of its rainbow trout. There were salmon again
through the length of the Bella Coola River, but again it
was the Indians who caught them, not Mackenzie and his

French Canadian voyageurs. In 1807, Simon Fraser traveled the full length of the great river named for him and so far as I know neither he nor his men fished for or caught a single fish, though they also were glad to get them from the natives.

After exploration the explorers settled in and became fur traders, and the change began. By 1811 David Harmon of the Northwest Company was awaiting the return of the salmon to Stuart Lake, far up the Fraser River. On August 22, he wrote: "One of the natives has caught a Salmon, which is joyful intelligence to us all, for we hope and expect in a few days to have abundance. They weigh from five to seven pounds. There are also a few of the larger kind, which will weigh sixty or seventy pounds."

New Caledonia, or north central British Columbia as it now is, was no easy land to survive in without fish, and the men of Fort Stuart and Fort St. James eagerly welcomed not only salmon, but whitefish, sturgeon, trout and carp. Though most of the leaders were Scotsmen, some presumably with memories of burn and loch trout in the Highlands, no one seems to have thought of rod and line; and Governor Simpson found John Tod half-starved at Fort McLeod when he might well have been taking grayling by the score in the Pack and Parsnip rivers.

Down at the headwaters of the Columbia David Thompson, still exploring, carefully noted the habits and characteristics of the five species of salmon, but was content to barter for supplies of them from the Indians. He himself hunted wild horses and mountain goats and sent his men out into the hills in search of other game, not always with too much success: "Amongst Hunters who depend wholly

on the chase, there sometimes comes a strange turn of
mind; they are successful and everything goes well; a
change comes, they either miss, or wound the Deer, without getting it; they become excited and no better success
attends them, despondency takes place, the Manito of the
Deer will not allow him to kill them; the cure for this is a
couple of days' rest; which strengthens his mind and body."

A perceptive man, Thompson, and a true philosopher and
poet. He was also observant, enthusiastic and a wonderful
gatherer of local knowledge; he would have made an ideal
fisherman—in fact of all the explorers he would certainly
have been the one most likely to make something of the
virgin possibilities of the country. But the sad truth is that
he seems never to have tried it.

For long after Thompson's day the fur traders of the
Columbia district seem to have remained careless of the
possibilities of the salmon runs, whether for food or recreation. Governor Simpson of the Hudson's Bay Company
read them an irritable lecture in 1824. "The good people
of the Spokane District, and I believe of the interior of
Columbia generally, have shown an extraordinary predilec-
tion for European Provisions without once looking at or
considering the enormous price it costs. . . . I do not
know any part of the Country on the East side of the
Mountain that affords such resources in the way of living
as the Spokane District; they have abundance of the finest
Salmon in the World, besides a variety of other fish within
100 yards of their door, plenty of Potatoes, Game if they
like it; in short everything that is good or necessary for an
Indian trader; why therefore squander thousands uselessly
in this manner?"

Simpson's words, as usual, had an immediate effect. He was a governor who made himself felt from Montreal to Fort Vancouver and back again without ever raising his voice. Within five years Fort Langley on the Fraser was buying seven or eight thousand fish a year at a cost of something under a cent apiece. Within ten years the Hudson's Bay Company was shipping four thousand barrels of salt salmon a year to the Hawaiian Islands and claiming the fishery as a monopoly.

Just who was the first sportsman to take Pacific salmon on rod and line, it is hard to say. Frank Forester seems to think that some of the California miners of the '49 gold rush may have found time for it. The first man who wanted to try it in British Columbia met with disappointment. He was Captain John Gordon of *H.M.S. America,* who visited Fort Victoria around the time of the Oregon boundary dispute in 1845. Roderick Finlayson, the Hudson's Bay factor at Victoria, gave the Captain salmon for breakfast one day and Gordon instantly recognized a chance of sport. Finlayson has left at least two accounts of the result, both substantially the same, though with varying dialogue: "The Captain was preparing his fishing rod to fish for salmon with the fly, when I told him the salmon would not take the fly, but were fished here with bait. I then prepared fishing tackle with bait for him, after which he went in a boat to the mouth of the harbor and fished several fine salmon with the bait. His exclamation on his return was: 'What a country, where the salmon will not take the fly.' "

Here then was our sophisticated (and somewhat irritable) fisherman, coming to the virgin country, thoroughly misguided by local information, completely missing a fine

opportunity. Which was bad enough in itself; but legend
has blamed Gordon's disgust with the unsporting salmon
for the loss of Oregon Territory to British Columbia. The
story is that he readily convinced the commissioners that
a country whose salmon behaved so contemptibly simply
wasn't worth arguing about, though the fact seems to be
that Gordon got back to England too late for his reports
to have influenced anyone at all, if indeed he made any
reports.

Whether or not Gordon used a rod for his boat fishing is
not quite clear. In one account Finlayson suggests he used a
handline, in the one I have quoted here he leaves it wide
open. But there is no doubt about another much more important historical character who arrived in British Columbia
almost exactly a hundred years ago as I write this: Matthew
Baillie Begbie, the great bearded judge who controlled the
miners through the Fraser and Cariboo gold rushes and laid
the firm foundations of law in the province.

In March of 1859, less than five months after his arrival,
Begbie noted in a dispatch to Governor Douglas from New
Westminster: "The face of the country is being gradually
better known, although very little cleared. Two trout
streams have been discovered; one running into the right
side of the bay opposite the shoal; the other nearly opposite
Tree island. The latter runs for a considerable distance, apparently, parallel to the Pitt river and issues, like the Pitt,
from a lake in the mountains."

The judge went on to draw some conclusions about the
nature and topography of the country, as no doubt was
seemly in a semiofficial report to the Governor. But he was
putting first things first. He had discovered not just two

streams or brooks or water courses or little rivers, but two
trout streams, the Brunette and the Coquitlam as they later
were called, and no doubt the statement was properly based
on incontrovertible evidence—that he had caught trout in
them.

Through the next thirty years Judge Begbie strode and
rode the length and breadth of the land, carrying the law
in his saddlebags and seldom missing a chance to hunt or
fish. Long Bacheese, the magnificent Déné hunter who led
Dunlevy to the first rich gold find in the Cariboo country,
was the judge's guide in the interior and soon had his name
changed to Begbie Ba'tiste. Around Victoria, an old Lin-
colnshire poacher steered him through the grouse country
and the duck sloughs and repeatedly encouraged him to
break the game laws. And in other parts of the country his
faithful magistrates, Cox, O'Reilly, Ball, Haynes and many
others, themselves sportsmen almost to a man, stood by to
tip him off to a newly discovered trout lake or stream, a
good crop of grouse or a worthwhile flight of ducks and
geese.

They had fine sport, these gentlemen, whether they were
chasing coyotes with foxhounds, deceiving trout in the
streams, kicking up grouse from the poplar swales or starting deer on the mountain slopes. With them the golden age
of natural sport in British Columbia began. It had taken
time, just as the discovery of the land itself had taken time,
but it has lasted well—only this year I have found a new
summer steelhead stream that disturbs my winter dreams,
and there are others yet to be tried.

I had not meant to follow the matter through quite so
thoroughly when I started on it. But I think I have con-

vinced myself that the angler set down in a primitive wilderness, even a sophisticated and well-equipped angler, would not have found sport much better, quite probably not as good, as we find it today. Those dour old Scotsmen of the Northwest Company and the Hudson's Bay Company, with their canoes and equipment and their wonderful French Canadian canoe-men, were the ones who had the perfect chance. But it seems they were too busy keeping alive or making a dollar for the company to use it; or else they were too canny to put anything down in the record where the fearful eye of Governor Simpson might come upon it. Dr. Cheadle and Lord Milton, the first overland tourists, carried guns on their famous journey in 1863. But they shot only for the pot and even so were dangerously close to starvation as they hacked their way down the North Thompson.

The dream of primitive and unspoiled abundance is a little like old age's dream of youth. "Oh, to be twenty again," says age, then follows with the immediate corollary: "But only knowing what I know now and understanding as I now understand." The idea is perfect. But the execution of it might have proved altogether too difficult.

2. *The Indian and Me*

WHEN *Fisherman's Spring* WAS PUB-
lished in 1951, it was reviewed in one of the great U.S.
weekly news magazines. The reviewer was kind and gener-
ous, even flattering. But he was not a fly-fisherman and it
was plain that my concern for the finer points of the sport
disturbed him a little. He concluded that an Indian, watching me at work, might wonder just who was caught, the
fish or the fisherman.

I suppose it is natural to assume that North American
Indians and other primitive peoples were relentless and
efficient pursuers of fish and game. But the truth is far
otherwise. The Indians of the Pacific Northwest were the
salmon people; salmon fed them and made them rich; salmon gave them leisure in which to develop arts and crafts
and an intricate social organization. In return they har-
vested the salmon, and other fish as well, with religious respect; they bound themselves with rigid traditions and con-
ventions in the fishing; and they dreamed up ichthyological
superstitions that leave the most romantic conceptions of
the angler far behind.

Some of the Indian peoples believed that the salmon
came from a human village far out in the ocean. The people
of this village transformed themselves into salmon and swam
to the rivers to bring food to the people who lived by
them. So only the meat of the fish must be used—the rest,

the whole skeleton, must be returned to the river to go back
to the ocean village and take on its human form again. Not
a bone nor a fin must be missing or the restored human form
would be proportionately deformed.

How many of the Indians believed this, I am not sure.
I should judge not many; it sounds more like one of the
tales told over the winter fires and feasting in the long
houses. But there isn't the slightest reason to doubt that
they all saw something supernatural in the unfailing return
of the salmon, and were properly grateful for it. The first
fish of the season was always greeted with special ceremonies. Fishing stopped at once. The fish itself was placed
on the rocks beside the river, its head pointing upstream
to show the way to the others. Later it would be cut up and
cooked according to the established ritual of the tribe and
divided among all the members; the skeleton would be
returned to the river. Only when ritual and tradition had
been fully observed would the fishing start again.

This was only the beginning. Taboos and ceremony were
observed at all stages of the fishing and often interfered
with it. The early explorers, who were very practical men,
were quite critical of some of the Indian ways. Alexander
Mackenzie, the first man to cross the full width of the
continent to the northwest Indian lands, wrote of the Bella
Coolas in 1793: "These people indulge an extreme superstition respecting their fish, as it is apparently their only
animal food. Flesh they never taste, and one of their dogs
having picked and swallowed part of a bone which we had
left, was beaten by his master until he disgorged it. One of
my people also having thrown a bone of the deer into the
river, a native, who had observed the circumstance, imme-

diately dived and brought it up and, having consigned it to the fire, instantly proceeded to wash his polluted hands."

The chief would not allow Mackenzie and his men to take venison with them in the canoes "as the fish would instantly smell it and abandon them so that he, his friends and relations must starve." The Indians would give the white men only cooked salmon and would not allow them to go near the place where the salmon were cleaned and prepared; nor would they let them dip water from the river in an iron kettle but gave them wooden boxes "because salmon dislike the smell of iron."

That great and good man David Thompson, who first discovered and mapped the sources of the Columbia and first followed the full length of that noble river to the sea, spent some time in 1811 with the Indians who were spearing salmon at Kettle Falls. Thompson was a close and sympathetic observer of Indian ways and he makes it clear that the Columbia River fishermen knew a great deal about their salmon. They knew, for instance, that there were five distinct species, each of which used a different spawning area; they knew that salmon do not feed in fresh water and that all of them, regardless of species, die after spawning. "The arrival of the salmon throughout this River," Thompson says, "is hailed with dances and many ceremonies . . . deep attention is paid by [the natives] to what they believe will keep the Salmon about them; for this purpose the Beach of the River is kept very clean, no part whatever of the Salmon is allowed to touch the River after it is brought on shore, the scales, the bowels &c. are all cleaned on the land a few yards from the River, for experience has taught them the delicate perceptions of this fish; even a Dog going in the edge of the water, the Salmon dash down the Current, and any part of them being thrown into the water, they do not return until the next day, especially if blood has been washed; in spearing of them, if the fish is loose on the Spear and gets away, the fishing is done for that day."

We know today that salmon are sensitive to water-borne scents, perhaps especially so at a fishway or fall; a certain extract from the skin of humans and other mammals will turn fish away and delay their return for thirty or forty minutes. But there is nothing to suggest they are unduly sensitive to the remains of their own kind or that they would be disturbed for a whole day by a repulsive odor; the practices of the Kettle Falls people hardly agree with the widespread custom in other tribes of returning the skeletons of dead salmon to the rivers. But Thompson, who was a most careful observer and a very honest recorder, seems to have felt there was some sense in them.

"I looked on part of the precautions of the Natives as so much superstition," he adds, "Yet I found they were not so; one of my men, after picking the bone of a Horse about 10 A.M. carelessly threw it in the river, instantly the Salmon near us dashed down the current and did not return until late afternoon; an Indian dived, and in a few minutes brought it up, but the fishery was over for several hours."

This matches Mackenzie's experience with the Bella Coolas, five or six hundred miles away and twenty years earlier. But I'm not sure it makes much more sense than does the angler who spits on his bait for luck or refuses to go out on a falling barometer. Thompson was more critical of some of the other taboos.

"The spearing of the Salmon at the Fall," he says, "was

committed to one Man for the Public Good, [so] of course
the supply was scant until the fish became sufficiently numerous to use the Seine Net. The third day we were here,
the Spearman in going to the Fall with his Spear came close
to the bleached skull of a Dog, this polluted his Spear; he
returned to his shed, informed them of the accident, and to
prevent the fish going away he must purify himself and his
Spear; this was done by boiling the bark of the red Thorn,
the steam of which on himself and the head of his Spear
began the process. When the heat had moderated, his face
and hands and the Spear were washed with it and by noon
he was ready and proceeded to the Fall. . . . The River at
these Falls is about 300 yards wide and from the immense
numbers [of salmon] that ascended these Falls from Sun
rise to its setting might have employed at least thirty spear-
men, and why only one was employed I never could learn."

So much for the Indian as an entirely practical and
deadly fisherman. No doubt there was a reason, and a good
one, for the single spearman. Perhaps there was an agree-
ment with other tribes farther upstream, though there were
not many of them. Perhaps it was a conservation measure
that permitted the early fish to get through in good numbers and maintain their run. Perhaps it was a hereditary
right of some kind, its sanctions lost in the remote history
of the tribe.

It is difficult to say how conscious the Indians were of
the need for conservation—of the importance of allowing
at least a proportion of the runs to reach the spawning beds
and carry out their purpose. The spirit of conservation was
in the respect they showed the fish and the practical effect
of conservation was in a great many of the taboos and re-

straints they imposed upon themselves. Quite certainly, they could have caught up the entire runs to many of the smaller streams had they chosen to do so and, just as certainly, they did not. It seems more than likely that from time to time wise men of the tribes saw the need for restraints, translated these into stories and dances and ceremonies, and established taboos which became secure and permanent tradition. Some may have been more effective than others in ensuring a proper escapement of spawners for the perpetuation of the race; but that is just as true of the modern taboos set forth in fishery regulations.

Perhaps it was not just my concern for the traditions of fly-fishing that bothered my reviewer. Perhaps it was my attitude towards the fish themselves and the other wildlife of the streams. Here again I would argue that I am rather closer to the spirit of the primitive Indian than might be supposed, though I am rather less of a sentimentalist. When Alexander Mackenzie was passing through the Peace River Country on his journey to the Pacific he was approached by an Indian who asked for a cure for a sickness of the joints of his legs and thighs. The man was badly crippled and explained that he had practically lost the use of his legs for five winters past. This evil, he was convinced, had come upon him because of his cruelty in killing a bitch wolf and her whelps. He had found them in an old beaver lodge, had set fire to the lodge and burned them alive. As I recall the rest of the story, Mackenzie administered a rather painful treatment that the Indian prescribed for himself and the poor man improved considerably.

Then there was Long Bacheese, the Déné Indian who guided Dunlevy and Sellars and their partners to the first strike of coarse gold on the Fraser River system in the summer of 1859. Bacheese spoke a little French and English and worked for the Hudson's Bay Company, so he was not a true primitive. He was a huge and very powerful man, a superb archer and an infallible hunter. He preferred to hunt stark naked except for a loincloth and seemed to his white companions to be able to disappear into the woods and reappear from them without sound or effort, a three-dimensional shadow of muscle and bone and sinew. Each morning, before they were awake, he slipped out of camp and brought back a deer which was cut up and roasted for breakfast. It was always a doe because, he told them, the bucks were "sick inside, this moon. Not sick, just look sick. White man see, not like, no eat."

One morning, as they sat at breakfast, Jim Sellars picked a bone and threw it in the fire. Bacheese checked him immediately: "Non, non," he said. "Not burn good bone. Dog eat bone. No dog here, but mebbe wild tillicum. Find bone, eat. Good. Coyote all time come behind where man go. Hungry, find bone, eat. Tell Indian thank you."

Still sitting there, Bacheese threw back his head and howled like a coyote. From a distance, one here, one there, the wild coyotes answered him. Bacheese looked at his friends. "You see?" he asked quietly.

This splendid giant was so far beyond the average of his people in hunting skill and efficiency that he seems like a being from another world. Though he showed a ready instinct for sport when it came to proving his bow against the rifles of the miners or wrestling and running foot races with them, he hunted primarily for meat and not for sport. Yet he had his own carefully guarded rules and sanctions and achieved as a result of them the powerful sense of affinity with wild creatures that most sportsmen seek.

Then there is my friend Jonah Cole, a Hoh River Indian who lives near Quinault Lake on the Olympic peninsula. Jonah is one of the few Indians still able to take charge of an ocean-going canoe, to force it out against the breakers, guide it through the combers of a Pacific storm and bring it safely to the beach again through the violence of surf and ground swell. He is proud of this and speaks of it quite often. Yet the Quinaults and the Hoh River people were never confirmed whale hunters like the Makahs and the Nootkas, farther north along the coast. A few of them used to go out after whales, but they were the exceptional bold spirits who sought honor and glory and the thrill of the hunt rather than the material returns. I suppose it is many years now since even the Nootka and Makah canoes brought home the last whales killed in the old way. So I was curious about Jonah's deepwater excursions.

"You don't hunt whales, do you?" I asked him.

"No," he said. "Not any more."

"Then what do you go out for? Seals and sea lions?"

"Sometimes," Jonah said. "For fun, mostly."

He told me of the difficulties of bringing a canoe to shore through the surf, of an upset with a green crew and a three-hour struggle as the canoe drifted in and out through the brutal pounding of the breakers. I knew then what he meant by "fun," for I have talked the same way myself of storms weathered and canoes upset in bad places. White man's talk, I thought, and a white man's view of things. But I knew in a moment I was wrong. It is universal talk, exactly the same talk as Jonah's forebears brought in from the whale hunts and no small part of the reason they went out in the first place and found the strength and courage to strike the whale and handle the cedar-bark ropes and the sealskin floats. It is simply the talk of a man who has tested himself against considerable natural hazards and come safely and successfully through them.

Jonah is also a great elk hunter and depends on the elk for much of his meat. But his greatest memory of an elk hunt goes back to a day in 1917 when he and some other young fellows got hold of a jug of wine and went out in pursuit of one of the Quinault herds. Somehow they drove the herd into the water, with the river high, just above a log jam. One young Indian got up there ahead of Jonah and shot seven of the elk. Jonah came up to him and said, "That's enough"—then shot ten more himself.

Jonah told me the story as we sat on a gravel bar by Eagle's Lake Pool on the Quinault, and it had a certain shock value.

"What did you do with them all?" I asked. "How did you get them out?"

Jonah hesitated a moment and his answer was not as easy as his telling of the story had been. "There was enough meat for the whole village," he said. "Four canoe loads of meat."

Perhaps so. But a five- or six-hundred-pound elk rolled under a log jam by a powerful current is not easily recovered, even by strong young Indians, and I suspect that most of the slaughtered seventeen were lost. The happening remains one of Jonah's great memories not because of the meat, but because of the companionship, the jug of wine, the excitement of the hunt and the fierce delight of the killing. It was a young man's deed, excessive and wasteful and not without its shame. But it is a powerful memory after forty years because of its dramatic values, not because there was plenty to eat later on.

Jonah is a skillful trout fisherman. With an old steel rod and a level-wind casting reel he can spot a lure anywhere he wants; under bushes and overhanging limbs, up against logs and snags, behind a rock or into a distant eddy. He tends his tackle, his canoe and the rest of his gear as any self-respecting sportsman or Indian should, and with just that extra shade of unnecessary care that we both know is needed to propitiate the spirits that guard and guide us. I don't think he owns a fly rod or uses one very often, but when we are out together he is likely to pick up one of mine and handle it very adequately. "Fly-fishing!" he will say at such times. "That's *sport*."

Men may be raised differently, under different philosophies, with different needs and different values. But hunting and fishing are only less universal than hunger and love and death. I have recognized the same light in the eye of an Araucanian Indian in Chile when we worked for a big rainbow as lighted the face of Peter the Eskimo when we hooked a grayling or an arctic char in the Coppermine, or dropped a wolf with a long shot on the tundra. It is there in the eyes of my friend Gilbert Cook, the Kwakiutl, when he talks of taking his seine boat outside next season to find the homing sockeye salmon—not with a long net and blind sets, but with the short net of the inside waters and cunning sets close inshore where he knows the fish run through. It is there too, bright and plainly to be recognized, in the eyes of many friends who cannot claim a drop of Indian blood, as we talk of how the fish will rise or the birds fly—in the eyes of men from Madison Avenue, the university cloister, the courts of law, the machinist's bench, the store counter and the logger's claim.

It should not be too surprising then that the Indian and the white sportsman have so many ways in common. When the Haida Indian carves the manikin on his halibut hook and is careful not to insult the fish by making the hook too small, he is brother to the man who searches out a pair of tiny blue chatterer feathers to finish the dressing of an Atlantic salmon fly. Both know the uncertainty of the search ahead, both recognize the fallibility of scientific understanding, whether it be biological or shamanistic. Both feel the need to propitiate the hunted and each in his way seeks to build the prestige of his quarry.

But above and beyond this is tradition, the faithful following of our fathers and forefathers. We follow with a certain rigidity, because the old ways have proved themselves in satisfactions and successes. Yet because the tradition is a live one, in constant use, we accept change and develop new tradition in each generation. The father of today's fisherman accepted, not without reluctance, the tapered silk line in place of tapered horsehair, the cane rod in place of greenheart and lancewood. Just as slowly we turn today to modern synthetic lines in place of silk, and with even greater reluctance to rods of Fiberglas instead of cane. The reluctance is wholly proper. The advantages of new tools and new ways may be obvious; but we must also be certain that they do not impair or detract from the ancient satisfactions.

With a similar hesitation, the primitive whaler learned to tip his harpoon with iron instead of mussel shell and replaced his cedar-bark lines with hemp. No doubt some early Queequeg clung to the mussel shell long after the coming of steel and no doubt the young bloods, watching his triumphs, wondered whether the bright new metal lacked some virtue of the sharp and brittle shell—perhaps an affinity with the whale's heart. For it is the imponderable and the unpredictable in the ways of wild creatures that unites us and makes our common ways. We try to become one with the creature we pursue, to know its ways and anticipate its actions. Because we are different and apart, hedged in by the power of reason and man's way of thinking, we can never wholly succeed. If we could, we should kill the light that kindles in the eyes, the thrill that stirs muscle and heart and brain; and half the satisfaction of man in his own prowess would be forever lost.

In his primitive time, and often still today, the Indian seeks to propitiate the gods and enlist their aid to his greater success, because his tools are limited. When I choose to limit my tools and go out on the water or into the hills, I bring myself into dealing with those same gods; my means of propitiation are little changed and my triumphs are as readily comprehensible to my Indian brother as his to me.

PART THREE

The Home River

1. *Defined*

Most anglers have a parent stream and a home river, which may or may not be one and the same. The parent stream is the river of youth, the scene of boyhood endeavors, successes and failures; it nursed him and taught him and in large measure formed the angling side of his character. The home river of his later years may be this same stream, changed much or little by the passing of time, the hand of man or its own flow; or it may be another stream altogether, in some near or distant part of the world to which his life has taken him. All that really matters is that it should be the stream he knows best, fishes most regularly and has adopted as his own.

Whether it be the stream of youth or the adopted stream of later years, a fisherman's home river (or it may be a home lake or some favorite bay in salt water) is of ultimate importance to him. It is a known, familiar place, full of memories and associations. It is well-beloved, or he would not have persisted in it. It may yield fish freely or grudgingly. It may produce large fish or small ones. It may be difficult or easy. These things don't really matter. Any good fish from it is worth a dozen better and larger fish from some distant place, because it has been caught under known conditions and standards. Any new discovery is an impressive triumph. The measure of a disaster can be exactly calculated. For this is the true testing ground. What a man achieves remains his own, to be matched against achievements in the past and others in the future. Everything that happens on the home stream builds and increases and enriches knowledge until it becomes intimacy. Yet since weather is weather, water is water and fish are fish, knowledge is never complete. Instead, the standard changes and one seeks still greater intimacy.

My own home river is the Campbell on Vancouver Island, beside which I have now lived for twenty-five years. It heads in the high mountains of Strathcona Park and used to come down through three good-sized lakes to the two-hundred-foot drop of Elk Falls, some two and a half miles from the salt water of Discovery Passage.

This last two and a half miles is now all that is left of
the Campbell proper, as I shall explain shortly. But in any
case, this is the part I call my home stream and with which
I am mainly concerned at the moment. It is a good-sized
river, averaging two or three hundred feet in width and
with a mean annual flow of some twenty-five hundred
cubic feet a second—which means that at low water one
can, or could, wade across it with ease at two or three
places; at average water, only with difficulty and some
skill. It has no sizable resident fish—every fish worth catching has spent some time in salt water. The chief migrants
are steelhead and cutthroat trout, king and coho salmon;
dog and humpback salmon and a few Dolly Vardens also
use the river, but these are of no direct importance to the
fisherman.

I have written of all this before, in detail and at length.
But because it is my home stream I have also fished it a
good deal since I last wrote of it. And within the last ten
years it has been changed almost out of recognition. So
there is a good deal new to write about.

First, of the changes. Shortly after the war a hydroelectric dam was built just above Elk Falls and a second
dam, for storage purposes, near the foot of Lower Campbell Lake. The first dam directed the river into penstocks,
which fed it to the powerhouse at the foot of the canyon,
some three-quarters of a mile below Elk Falls. The second
dam raised the level of Lower Campbell Lake by fifty-
eight feet and flooded out the several miles of the stream
between there and the Upper Lake. The third stage of the
project, completed only a year or two ago, is a dam below
the foot of Upper Campbell, raising that lake over a hun-

dred feet, backing it up to Buttle Lake in Strathcona Park
and raising the level of Buttle nineteen feet. This has effectively drowned out the rest of the river between the upper
and lower lakes, the whole of the Buttle River, several
miles of excellent water on the Elk River and the lower
reaches of all the attractive streams that flow into Buttle
Lake. It has also destroyed the whole of Buttle Lake's
beautiful shoreline and with it the main values of Strathcona Park; it has made a splendid natural valley into a grim
reservoir between the timbered mountains, with only the
scars of draw-down to mark its edge; it has—but why go
on? The total of destruction has been prodigious, and all
to produce industrial power at six mills per kilowatt, which
could far better have been done with two or three strategi-
cally placed thermal plants. It is an economic travesty and
a land-use tragedy, but it concerns us little here except in
its effects on the last two miles of river below the powerhouse outlet.

These effects have been gradual, over a period of about
ten years, as storage has increased behind the dams and
more and more turbines have been brought into produc-
tion. There are six of them altogether at the main powerhouse, each one using seven hundred cubic feet of water a
second. So the summer flow of the river has built up from
its former average of around four to six hundred cubic
feet a second to a normal level of just over four thousand
cubic feet a second in the summer of 1958. At this level the
Campbell is a big and powerful stream. Every lie is
changed, in character if not in position. Wading most of
the pools, especially when working upstream with a dry
fly, has become hard work. And one has to search a much

larger area of more difficult water for what remains, so far, the same number of fish.

This is not necessarily discouraging—in fact it is exciting and challenging. Logically, though I am not at all sure it has worked out so far, the increased flow of water should produce larger runs of fish. Spawning areas are more extensive and better protected. The usual low water periods in the freezing weather of January and February should no longer occur. Excessive floods at time of heavy rain and snow melt should be materially reduced. All these factors should make for a larger and more successful hatch of fish.

It is difficult to understand why these improvements have not already produced a marked improvement in the runs of humpback and tyee salmon, which go down to salt water almost immediately after hatching and return only as fully mature fish. Perhaps it will take a little more time. The runs of coho salmon, winter and summer steelhead and cutthroat trout are another matter. All these fish spend one or two years in fresh water before migrating to sea. In this again, the increased flow of the river should raise a larger crop of young fish by giving them wider range and greater quantities of food, but it does not seem to have happened. The winter steelhead run has fallen off very badly indeed; the run of big spawning cutthroats that always came up in late summer and early fall seems to have disappeared entirely; the coho salmon run has fallen off; only the summer steelhead, which never were very abundant, seemed to pick up a little, and I suspect that even they are falling off again.

There may be an explanation for this in several factors which tend to counterbalance the increased flow. Under its present control, the river fluctuates considerably as the power demand falls off over holidays and late at night; this probably destroys a good deal of small aquatic life and reduces the amount of food produced. The relatively swift and heavy flow of the river over much of its bed at the new normal level may also reduce the quantity of food. And, most important of all, the three-quarters of a mile of canyon water below Elk Falls is now dead, with only a slight seepage flow except at flood time, because all the water is passed around it in the penstocks. I believe the deep pools of the canyon were the most important rearing water on the river and this diversion of all flow from them represents a very serious loss.

After this rather gloomy account, it may seem foolish to go on fishing the river. But it is my home stream, it is close at hand, I find the changes fascinating to observe and the only way I can observe them is by fishing. Besides I do not think the story is yet complete. This is the first year we have had the full flow of six turbines almost constantly. Fluctuations to lower water levels have not been as drastic or as prolonged as in former years and are not likely to be so again. In that case the increased flow may compensate for the loss of canyon water. In time it should also produce small modifications in the bed of the river which will shelter fish better and produce more food. And it is quite possible that we may get increased runs of the types or races of fish that are best adapted to the changed conditions.

There are already some indications that this is happening. A small run of dog salmon which comes to the river in October has increased quite noticeably over the past few years—not necessarily a desirable thing. In the same period I am convinced there has been a slow increase of the summer steelhead run. This is a sparse run at best and one can never see the fish as one can the dog salmon, so the only test is by fishing. The years from 1951 to 1956 gave me good fishing for nice bright fish that ran from two and a half to nine pounds. In 1957 I could not get time to fish. In the year of 1958, summer fishing gave me only two fish of over three pounds, but an unusual number of fish running from three-quarters of a pound to just under two pounds, all bright little steelheads in from the sea and all maturing to spawn. A high proportion of these should survive to go to sea again and return as much larger fish.

These fish are a true grilse run—that is to say, they are both males and females returning to spawn after one year or less of sea feeding, and it seems reasonable to suppose that they are the by-product of a run of larger fish. Since the high water has changed many lies and made the river much harder to fish this summer, it is quite possible that the larger fish are there and I have not been able to find them. I know I have missed a number of rises from big fish, most of them because the increased current was carrying the fly too fast or with excessive drag.

This is a quick outline of the changes that have come to my home river in the last ten or twelve years. I hope and believe the last turbine is installed and that conditions will remain fairly stable from here on. But change will still go on for some years, the changes of the fish and other aquatic life as they adjust to the new conditions. What makes it all so interesting to the fisherman is that he too must change his methods and adapt his knowledge to the new conditions and the altered habits of the fish.

The changes in my home river have made a good many changes in my own ways of fishing and have brought me many experiences that were both exciting and revealing. In the next few chapters I shall try to describe some of these and show where they have led me, and the purpose of this short account is to set the scene in broad detail.

2. *The Beginnings of Change*

SOME EXTRAORDINARY THINGS HAPPENED
during the construction of the first dams on the Campbell
watershed. I remember one day asking an engineer in charge
of the work how he expected the water to spread from the
surge pool below the powerhouse—would it throw well
across the river to the left bank and run down both sides
of the big island or was it likely to hold to the right bank
and pour down along the south side of the island, leaving
the other side almost dry? He said he didn't know. I said
that if it all went down along the right bank there would
be some pretty drastic changes in the main spawning beds
of the tyee run. If this happened, would it be possible to
put in some sort of groin or baffle to spread the water properly? He said he supposed so, but no one had raised the
point.

That was when I first realized that no one in authority
had a watching brief for the fish and I began to worry,
though I wasn't quite sure what to worry about. Fortunately the fish had friends at court. One day in August of
the year the dam was being built, a construction foreman
stopped me on the road and asked if I knew how they were
going to close off the dam. I said I didn't.

"Then you ought to," he said. "They'll have the whole
river closed off for six weeks or better."

"They can't," I said. "The tyees are running in already. They can't anyway. Something's always running."

"Yes, they can. At the last stage they'll drop three twenty-foot gates in place, one after another. At the present flow of the river it'll take at least six weeks to fill up behind that and make any spill."

I thought of six weeks of dead and stagnant water in the great pools of the river, without even a trickle of live water between them. I thought of the huge salmon, dead without spawning, their bright bodies littering the bottoms of the pools; of others still trapped in salt water, milling hopelessly around the river mouth until the end of October. Then I went home and did some telephoning.

The result was a delay in construction while three twenty-four-inch valves were brought up from the State of Washington and installed in the face of the dam. These kept a flow of water through the pools—not much, but enough—while the gates were installed. The salmon survived, schooled shoulder to shoulder in the aerated water at the heads of the pools. And when the rains came in mid-October they were still strong and alive to spread over the newly covered spawning beds and do their work. The construction foreman would probably prefer to remain anonymous, but I often think there should be a monument to him on Campbell River Spit, overlooking the tyee grounds, and every fisherman should make obeisance to it as he comes in with a fish to the weighing station.

From the fly-fisherman's point of view, the first big change in the river came about at the old Canyon Pool, where the powerhouse now stands and spews out turbine water into the surge pool. The Canyon Pool in the days before the dams was quite magnificent. The water came out between sheer rock walls into the body of the pool in smooth flow over a twenty- or thirty-foot depth. From there it spread evenly on either side and still smoothly into a broad fan that gradually shallowed, to break on the point of the island and into the rapids that run on either side of the island. Winter and summer steelhead came to it and lay faithfully over the broad tail where fly or lure could be swung gracefully across them; humpback and coho and tyee salmon came there, to wait their spawning time; and, above all, the harvest cutthroats came, great golden fish of two, three and four pounds. They showed first in late July, with or possibly just before the humpback salmon, and fresh fish kept moving in all through August.

There may be greater sea-run cutthroat pools than the old Canyon Pool, but I don't know of one. The fish lay best and took best in the glassy fantail of the pool, where the water, smooth as satin under the summer sun, began to gather speed as the pull of the rapid below sucked at it. Occasionally one rose or broke water; every so often three or four or half-a-dozen, not schooled but each on its own, cruised lazily up over the deeper water of the body of the pool and turned lazily back.

The pool fished best from the north bank, where one could wade over a deep channel and come up on a slightly shallower bar. The fish were not unduly shy, but they demanded respectful treatment. It was well to wade out without sending too much ripple ahead and even then to wait quietly on the bar a few minutes before starting to fish. It was important to cast lightly and accurately. A floating fly would get fair results; but a lightly dressed

Silver Brown on a well-greased line was better, more exciting and disturbed the pool rather less. It needed no more work than the smooth, gentle pull of the stealthy current. It might be taken with a swirl or a splash, but often the first warning was no more than a stop in the swing of the floating line.

Fishing in this way, half-a-dozen fish from two and a half pounds to just under four pounds was not an unusual catch for an August or early September afternoon. It was exciting, exacting, satisfying, and always uncertain. Once I killed a sixteen-pound steelhead and many times I broke 2x or 3x gut in striking unexpectedly solid fish—steelhead, I now suspect, though I did not realize then that the river had more than an occasional stray summer-run fish.

This wonderful fishing simply disappeared between seasons. One season it was there, the next it was not. The quiet summer flow of the river had been cut off by the dam, directed into the penstock and through the powerhouse into the surge pool, well over on the south side. No water at all came through the canyon and the smooth flow over the tail of the pool became dead water or at best a tame back eddy behind the runs that came from the lip of the surge pool.

It was hard to believe the fish were no longer there and I tried the dead water and the shallow glides just above the rapids for two or three seasons before I gave up. At first it was easy enough to wade upstream from the point of the island and fish the runs coming out of the surge pool. There were always fish there, but for some reason they were rainbows, not the thick-bodied, golden cutthroats of the old Canyon Pool. Then, as storage built up and more and more turbines came into service it became impossible to wade up and the water over the ledge along the north bank also became too deep for wading at all. As fly-fisherman's water it seemed that the Canyon Pool was finished. It was time to look for the harvest cutthroats elsewhere, and I thought at once of the Island Pools and other favorite places where I had caught them occasionally as they ran up. The search led me into a whole new wealth of fishing in my home river.

3. *The Search*

I HAD NEARLY ALWAYS FISHED FOR THE August cutthroats in the Canyon Pool with a greased line and a thinly dressed wet fly, drifted rather than worked, just under the surface of the water. This did not seem the ideal method for the broken water of the other important pools in the river and I began to look for something else.

Wading up into the runs from the surge pool, I had used floating flies—hair-winged Mackenzie River patterns on No. 10 hooks—and the fish came quite well to them. Going back down again I used greased line or a simple wet fly as a sort of control, and it began to seem fairly clear that the floating flies got more action, even though the fish were not always hooked. This made me think of searching for my lost cutthroat run with dry fly instead of wet.

There are certain disadvantages to searching with a floating fly, especially in a big fast stream. Wading upstream over a bottom of great round slippery rocks—and the Campbell has little else—is bad at any time, but doubly so if one must carry a fly in the air to keep it dry or keep a close eye on its float as one moves. Searching the likely spots takes many more casts than with a wet fly and much longer because each cast drifts only a straight line with the stream instead of sweeping across it. Above all, it is quite a trick to keep a fly floating well for any length of time in fast and broken water.

This last consideration turned my thoughts almost at once to larger flies. Bi-visibles, though they showed up well, would not float well enough for my purposes. The only dry flies I had larger than my Mackenzie patterns were some White and Gray Wulffs, which Lee Wulff had kindly sent me some while earlier. I had experimented with the White Wulffs at dusk off the creek mouths of a big lake, without too much success. In any case the Gray seemed a more likely fly, so I chose it to start my search.

How deliberate I was about all this, I cannot now remember. But if I know myself at all I imagine the thing grew on me by a series of lucky accidents rather than by deliberate planning. And the first of them happened at the pool just upstream from my house which I used to call the Nameless Pool and now call the Line Fence Pool.

Because it is close at hand I decided to use this pool for the first trial of the Gray Wulff, even though it was late August or early September and I had always considered the pool winter steelhead or spring cutthroat water rather than a prospect for late summer. It is a long shallow pool, with fairly strong current much broken by big rocks, and looks as though it would hold fish at a dozen different places, but I have never been able to find more than three or four regular lies.

I worked up with a big fly floating nicely and learned very quickly how awkward wading upstream among big slippery boulders can be. Only a few small fish rose at the fly and by the time I had passed the big rock and the last of the good lies, my enthusiasm for the new method was at a pretty low ebb and I was seriously considering reeling in and going home. Then a glassy glide along the edge of the rapid at the head of the pool insisted on another cast or two. After all, I was exploring and experimenting and plainly I had no business depending on nothing but the old proven places.

The sun was fairly well down and straight upstream, and the glide shone brilliantly. I pitched the fly up at the tail, a small fish took it down, I held the strike and got the fly back. I threw again, a little farther up and another fish rose to it; I almost held the strike again, but something about the rise suggested a better fish and I struck solidly into a handsomely colored little fifteen-inch cutthroat.

That was nice encouragement, even though it didn't prove much, so I put up another fly and threw it to the head of the glide. It floated beautifully and very briefly on the gleaming water, then there was a tiny rise and a broad glint of silver in an explosion on the smooth surface as I tightened. In the same moment the reel was running and scarcely a moment after that a bright three-pound steelhead was jumping in the pool fifty yards below me. The fast shallow water of the Line Fence Pool always gives a fish a chance to put on a big show. I had only 3x gut and wanted this one badly, so there were some anxious moments; but she came over the net at last and I had every encouragement to go on with the search for the missing fish.

The rest of that season, which I think was 1949, did not advance my search for the missing cutthroats by very much. But it convinced me that a floating fly, in spite of its difficulties, was good business and it showed me a lot of new places to look for fish. My notes are shamefully incomplete, but there was a day in the Main Island Pool, casting into the little runs that came over the bar, which produced six sea-run rainbows between one and two pounds

and a fifteen-inch cutthroat. A steelhead of eight or ten
pounds rose three times to the floating Wulff in the Lower
Island Pool and missed it each time. A real harvest cutthroat
of two and a half pounds rose twice and missed twice in
the Quinsam Pool; when he would not come again I offered a Silver Brown just under the surface and took him
at once.

Around and in between these successes, I began to suspect several things: first, and perhaps foremost, that either
the river had a considerably larger run of small summer
steelheads than I had previously suspected or else the
changed water conditions were doing something to increase the run. Secondly, it seemed that a floating fly stirred
more action, at least in the fast, rather shallow water I was
fishing, than a sunk fly. Thirdly, that I was missing a very
high proportion of rises or else the fish were missing the
fly. Fourthly, that summer steelhead of any size would,
under reasonably favorable conditions, come up to a floating fly. And finally that the frequently spectacular and
exciting nature of the fast water rises made this type of
fishing thoroughly worthwhile, even though a high proportion of the fish were not hooked.

I resolved to fish harder and more persistently in succeeding seasons, especially in July and August when the cutthroats should be running through, for I was still thinking
mainly in terms of cutthroats rather than of steelhead, large
or small. And I decided to tie some darker flies in the form
of the Wulffs—that is, with bulky hair wings split and set
well forward over the eye of the hook, a bulky tail of the
same material and rather sparse hackles. Nearly all creatures
of the Pacific Coast rainforest tend to be quite dark in
coloration, and it seemed possible that some of my missed

rises were caused by the rather pale colors of the standard
Gray Wulff. At the same time I was convinced that the
form of the fly, which left it supported on the water mainly
by wings and tail, with the body depressing the surface
film, was a big factor in stirring the fish. The success of the
rather large hook-size—No. 8—confirmed my previous experience in fishing floating flies for cutthroats and rainbows,
and I made up some of the new flies on No. 6's, to see how
far the theory could be carried.

These noble thoughts and good resolutions did not get
the results they might have, because I was not free to fish
very often during the next two summers. But I got out
enough to satisfy myself that the darker flies were good,
and No. 6 hooks were certainly not too large. The turbine
water was already beginning to build up by that time to
something over a thousand cubic feet a second, and the
Main Island Pool fished especially well, with a series of
runs coming off the long slanting bar and angling nicely
over towards the big main run on the far side. This encouraged me to believe that fish might hold better in it than
they had in the old days of really low summer water and
it also made a wonderful testing ground, since one could
wade up keeping well below the bar and search the runs
one after another.

There were a number of very sharp surprises in this
occasional fishing, and I should have taken more warning
from them than I did. For one thing, surprisingly large
fish were to be found at times lying in very shallow water
right up under the break of the bar. In 1950 a fresh steelhead of nine pounds took my floating fly with a perfect
head and tail rise in less than two feet of water. Fortunately
it was late in the season and I had a good big reel with

plenty of backing, so I managed to kill him without too much difficulty.

One August day in 1951 I was almost satisfied that I had found my lost cutthroats. It was a lovely sunny day and the water was just right, sparkling over the rocks of the bar in eight or ten firm little runs and spreading more smoothly into velvety dark green where the bar fell away to a depth of several feet. I floated a fly down the first run, watched its drift to the darker water almost opposite me— then saw a big fish come back in a rush, twenty or thirty feet down the run, just under the surface, turn and take the fly. Ten minutes later I had a perfect twenty-one-inch cutthroat in the net. In the next run or the one after, another cutthroat of just over twenty inches took the fly in a smooth quick rise, fought deeply and powerfully and also came at last to the net. Both these fish were over three pounds. In the main run from the bar I took two fish, one a cutthroat, one a small steelhead, both about eighteen inches. And in the quieter water between the main run and the heavy current under the far bank a very bright and lively steelhead of twenty-three inches came back at the fly with a fierce swirl away from me, jumped immediately and was securely hooked. My luck held and I beached her on the rocks at the tail end of the bar after an anxious ten or fifteen minutes.

This was an unusual day in that I missed or hooked lightly only three other fish of good size. One I knew was a cutthroat, one was a steelhead of well over twenty inches, the third was a fish I could not identify with any certainty. Every fish I did hook showed himself plainly as he rose and I was beginning to recognize the pattern of the "follow-back" rise. Surprisingly often I had noticed that big fish lying on the shallows would let the fly pass over them without a sign of having seen it, then suddenly appear from upstream, traveling down very fast for five, ten, twenty or even thirty feet to the fly. They always turned as they took it, still very fast, and kept moving just as fast after the take.

This meant it was vitally important to give the fly the longest possible drift and to recover line as quickly as one dared or could to keep pace with it without producing drag. If the fish turned towards the rod in his take, he could be hooked only by luck. If he turned away there was an excellent chance of hooking him, but one must be ready to let everything go the moment the hook was set.

All this was exciting and satisfying and delightful to the eye as fishing a wet fly rarely can be. It also fitted well with the pattern of behavior I expected of the fish. Both cutthroats and rainbows rise from the bottom, even in fairly deep water. For that reason they must come fast in fast water and are quite likely to miss. The follow-back rise, which I had noticed before, especially with rainbows on the Skagit River, seemed an extension of this principle—a delayed reaction partly because the fly was traveling fast, partly because the fish was not willing to expose itself over shallow water. If so, it argued that the big Wulff pattern flies were very powerful attractors.

Altogether I felt quite proud of my researches on that August day and very sure of my skill and adaptability on my home stream. It was the perfect build-up for a momentous set-back. What actually happened next was not a setback, but a most chastening and well-deserved shock to my pride and confidence.

4. *The Day Everything Happened*

Few honest fly-fishermen—and that, of course, is tautological, because all fishermen are honest, as our father Walton implied—can recall many days when everything they did was right and everything that happened went right. Most of my days are full of accidents and many of my triumphs have hung on threads much finer than 4x gut. But there was one day in my search of the changing Campbell that I shall always remember. Everything about it went almost right and nearly everything I did, except one thing, was done as well as I could do it. It should have been a day of immense triumph. Instead it was a day of many disasters. I remember it at least as vividly as any fishing day of my life, and with delight—though still with a sense of frustration. And I can readily recognize it now as the turning point of my struggle to understand my changing river.

This was an early September day, still in 1951, bright and sunny and with the river in perfect shape. I managed to get away at about three in the afternoon for what I thought would be a quiet hour or two in the Main Island Pool.

In spite of the rather high proportion of small—and occasionally large—steelheads I had happened on in the pre-

vious two or three summers, I was still thinking in terms
of cutthroats. I was fishing for cutthroats, expecting to find
cutthroats and geared for cutthroats. Now a cutthroat, even
a cutthroat fresh from the sea and of good size, is generally
rather a slow and dogged fighter. He does not often run
wildly or jump repeatedly and he rarely takes out more than
ten or fifteen yards of backing in his longest run; quiet and
careful handling will usually bring him to terms within the
length of a thirty-five-yard fly line.

I don't say I had weighed all this before I started out—
I didn't need to; I knew it in my bones after twenty-five
years of fishing for cutthroats. So it never occurred to me
to worry about my reel. The line I wanted was on a little
narrow drum Hardy Uniqua which just held it with some
twenty yards of fine backing. I took the little reel along
without the least hesitation—in fact with some satisfaction,
because it nicely balanced the Lambuth spiral rod I in-
tended to use.

The day was pleasant, as I have said already, and the
water was perfect. I started in at the lower end of the bar
in the Main Island Pool with 2x gut and a new fly pattern—
a variation of the Mackenzie River Brown and Yellow Bug,
tied Wulff fashion with fox squirrel wings and tail on a
No. 6 hook.

I began fishing at the very first ripple that could be considered a holding spot, right down near the tail of the bar,
as I had trained myself to do in case any fish should be
foolish enough to lie there in the bright sunlight. It was an
exercise to make sure my gear was all working right rather
than a cast made to catch a fish. But a fish rose almost as
the fly landed, a good one, and I missed him. He would

not come again, so I moved on and cast to the head of the
first real run. The fly danced back towards me, came over
the darker water. A broad-backed streak of brown and
silver came down after it, lunged at it and took it away in
an upstream run as sudden as an explosion. He jumped three
or four times, still running, then turned downstream in the
heavy current. He jumped again, handsomely silver and the
reel was still running when the 2x leader broke at the fly.

I was shaken, but not warned. I simply tied on another
fly and went on with the job. Another good fish rose in the
same run, but I missed him and he would not come again.
In the next run my fly disappeared in a perfect head and
tail rise and I was fast in a fish exactly like the one that had
broken me. He fought with the same violence and determination, but just a fraction more slowly. Somehow he
always stopped short of taking out all my backing, though
twice he turned when there were no more than a few feet
left on the reel; somehow I got him into the net, clutched
net and fish against my waders and stumbled to dry land.
He was a perfect fresh-run steelhead, twenty-three inches
long and four and a half pounds. I was so shaken I tried to
kill him with a rap on the head from my pipe, as I would
a one-pound trout. All that did was break the pipe and
persuade me to take stock for a moment.

Here I was, less than halfway up the pool, not even into
the best of the water yet. I had risen four fish, all good
ones, missed two, broken in one and killed one more by
luck than good management. Clearly this was a day of
days and heaven only knew what lay ahead of me in the
rest of the pool. I had nothing heavier than 2x gut and it
was quite obvious that the little reel simply wasn't up to

the job; in the first place it didn't carry enough backing and in the second place the friction of the ratchet alone, without any help from me, was enough to break 2x gut when a strong fish was running with only a few turns left on the spindle. The smart thing to do was go home and get another reel. Against that I had an appointment to be met in less than two hours. I dried my fly and went on to my fate.

It came very promptly. The next run I had to fish was what I call the second main run, and perhaps the most dependable lie in the pool. It is quite a wide run and I drifted the fly some half-a-dozen times without a rise. Then, in the broken water right up on the shallows, an enormous head and back and tail rolled out and the fly was gone—engulfed. So slow, so calm, so dignified was that rise that I had plenty of time to admit to myself that I was thoroughly scared to set the hook. But I did set it and the effect was immediate and awesome. The fish went away like a bullet, straight upstream and the poor little reel screamed its heart out. He jumped forty or fifty yards upstream and came back just as fast, without the slightest pause. Somewhere opposite me he turned and the next thing I knew he was jumping by a brush pile under the far bank. Then he was back again, almost at my feet. I cranked the reel frantically, caught up at last and tightened on him again. That was all he needed. He ran down and across this time, still just as fast, still jumping, towards the deepest part of the pool where I couldn't possibly follow. I touched the reel to try and slow him and that was the end; it was also the end of the backing—there weren't half-a-dozen turns left on the spindle when I looked.

I knew then that I was completely out of my league on my own home stream. Here were fish, big beautiful fresh-run fish, begging to take and be taken, and I just couldn't handle them. I was shaken not only metaphorically, but physically. And I shook physically. My hands shook, my knees shook and I was breathing as though I had climbed a mountain. As soon as I was partially recovered I broke my 2x leader back to what I judged to be 9/5 or about double its previous breaking strain. Then I did the same with another leader and tied the two together to give me a reasonable length again. Then I put up another fly.

While I was going through this performance I had seen what I very seldom see in the Campbell, another good big steelhead break water. I covered him and nothing happened until the fly had drifted ten or twelve feet past him. Then he came back after it, very fast, right along the top of the water, and took going away. He was considerably smaller than his partner, but just as wild and I treated him to all the pressure the rod would stand, which probably made him jump more. There was no question of netting him, but I worked him back down the length of the bar and finally got a finger in his gills and lifted him out. Just as bright and fresh as the first one and just over seven pounds.

That made me feel better and I went back for more. They were in the main run too; a wild fish of nine or ten pounds broke me with all the backing out; I missed one, perhaps two, and then killed a four-pounder. As nearly as I can remember the details, I had risen at least twelve good fish, all to the dry fly, had missed six or seven, been broken by three and killed three. So far as I know they were all steelheads—not a cutthroat among them.

Of course, I was up there again the next day, with all the right rigging. I searched the pool back and forth and up and down, but all I could find were two sixteen-inch fish—one a cutthroat, one a steelhead. It was quite clear that I had happened on a run of fish straight in from the sea; they had been holding briefly in the rather open water of the Island Pools and had passed on up—presumably to the deep pools in the canyon, which had a slight flow of water through it at that time.

Losing the run did not really matter, though it would have been nice to find them with a good big reel and plenty of backing. I promised myself that time would come on another day in another season. Meanwhile I was completely satisfied that under the right conditions summer steelhead would come better to a floating fly than to a wet fly; and from that day forward I found myself going out on the Campbell in the late summer and early fall months to look for steelheads first and cutthroats second.

Seven seasons have passed since that famous day and each year I have caught fewer of the big harvest cutthroats—in fact I don't think I have had a cutthroat of over three pounds, and not more than one or two over two pounds, in the past three seasons. Presumably the changing water conditions have had something to do with this, but I doubt if they are the whole story. Intensive fishing in the estuary and all over the river during the winter steelhead season, when the cutthroats are spawning, has taken a heavy toll. With salmon roe legal again and the average fisherman with spinning gear infinitely more effective than he used to be, it seems likely that very few fish manage to survive through the four years necessary to produce three-pounders.

But the summer steelhead are there every season and quite possibly in increasing numbers, though I cannot be sure of this. They are still hard to find and hard to predict, more like a few passing strays than a regular run, but they make wonderful sport for someone who lives on the river and can get out for an hour or two at pretty regular intervals between late July and late September. I miss the great golden cutthroats and still hope that I may one day find a few of them again. But the steelhead are more exciting fish and their wild fast water rises are as rough a test of the mixture of skill and luck that makes fishing as any man could want. And their fighting qualities are so extraordinary that they are worth a whole chapter to themselves.

5. *Speed and Stamina*

I HAVE ALWAYS FELT THAT FISHERMEN ARE inclined to exaggerate the performance of their favorite fish. Given a solid hook hold and reasonably appropriate gear, a man of decent skill should be pretty sure of bringing his fish to net or beach. A few times every season, through laziness or clumsiness or faulty judgment, I let fish break me. But this is always a surprise and once I know the hook is securely set I feel pretty confident about the outcome— except with the Campbell summer steelhead.

Since the day of reckoning in 1951, I have approached them with respect and with equipment that gives me a fair chance if I use it right. But I never feel too certain about landing one and nearly every fish I hook of three pounds and up gives me a number of moments when I do not expect to land him.

The chief difficulty remains in setting the hook, and there are good reasons for this. In the fast water the steelheads come at the fly wildly and unpredictably. Occasionally they roll out smoothly in perfect head and tail rises and when this happens I am nearly always able to set the hook solidly. Far more often they rise very suddenly and very fast, with a swirling turn which may be at the end of a long or short follow or may simply come straight up from the bottom. If the turn is towards me, I rarely hook the fish; if away from me I have something like an even chance.

Rather often, I suspect, the fish themselves miss the fly in these fast rises, though it is always carried under in the violence of the swirl.

Part of the reason for missing fish on these rises is the difficulty of recovering line when the fly is coming back on really fast water. From straight upstream one can do fairly well, but if the cast is at all across the current a careless recovery of line will produce drag, which also produces short rises. When one is searching a lot of water with rather few fish, the temptation is always to give the fly a good drift rather than risk interfering with it by trying to keep too tight a line. The possibility of a follow-back rise means that every cast should be given the longest possible drift and while one can delay drag by mending, the possibility of mending at all means there is a good deal of slack between the rod tip and the fly. I remember one three-pounder that came in a follow-back rise, swirled towards me and somehow hooked herself not thirty feet from the rod-top; she started jumping at once, still towards me and at an angle downstream, and had jumped five times before I was able to tighten on her. This was one of several such fish I have found with at least one mature, winged dragonfly in the stomach, which may partly account for the violence and type of the rise.

Drag is another cause of missed fish, but drag, whether deliberate or accidental, often rises fish that are not moved by a good natural drift, and a worthwhile proportion of the fish so risen are securely hooked. I avoid drag whenever I possibly can to reduce the number of missed fish, but am not above using it when I have worked over a good lie without response.

I sometimes wonder, after I have missed two or three good fish in succession, why I do not give them a chance at a wet fly instead. The main reason is that I am quite sure I would not rise nearly so many fish to a sunk fly, and I am not really sure I should hook a higher proportion. I very often do turn back downstream with a sunk fly after fishing up with a floater and more than once I have checked my results by immediately fishing up the same pool again with a dry fly. I have always had fewer rises to the sunk fly than the floater, which would be natural enough in the first two stages; but I think it is highly significant that on several occasions I have again had more rises to the floater on its second trip up the pool. I recall one day in the Main Island Pool when I rose seven fish going up with the dry fly, then rose two fish coming down with the wet, then rose four more going up again with the dry. But even if I were not convinced of this, I should still prefer the dry fly because the rises to it are so interestingly varied and show off the fish so beautifully. Many of these fast water rises have lasted far more vividly in my memory than anything that happened after them, whether the fish was hooked or not.

So much for the difficulties and excitements of the rise, which are quite enough to keep one keyed up to a lively pitch of expectation. What happens after the rise is nearly always explosive. There is absolutely no delay. The fish simply runs, usually jumping too, faster and farther than any fish I know of the same size.

I now use by preference for this fishing an eight-foot, four-ounce rod, though I occasionally go up to eight-and-three-quarters feet and five ounces in the hope that it will set the hook more certainly—which it never does. My reel is big enough to carry the fly line and at least a hundred yards of backing and the check is set as lightly as possible. My favorite leader is nine feet, tapered to 0x or .011″. My fly sizes are usually 6 or 8, though I have taken fish with flies tied on hooks as large as No. 2. My concern is to give the fish as much freedom as I possibly can from the moment the hook is set at least until his first run slows and stops.

Wild and unpredictable as they are, the fish have a certain pattern of performance. I think the three- and four-pounders are fastest of all and inclined to run straighter than the larger fish. Fish of over five pounds often turn in a wide circle on a drowned line, which is safe enough if everything is running freely, but sheer weight and power make them more dangerous in the final struggles on a short line.

The Main Island Pool, where I seem to hook most of the best performers, is an ideal place for them to put on a display. The bar which makes the head of the pool runs on a long slant upstream for 150 or 200 yards to the upper island. The lower end of the pool has filled in a good deal during the last few years of heavier flow from the surge pool, so most of the fish now lie well up along the bar. The body of the pool is all fast water, spreading from the very heavy runs at the head and probably nowhere much over six feet deep. A big rock breaks the water near the tail on the far side, though a fish can go thirty or forty yards beyond it without getting into the rapid below. Several other big rocks are near the center of the tail, right at the break into the rapids, and if a fish is determined to go out of the pool these are a real hazard unless he can be steered inside them. At the lower end of the bar is a little brushy island, where I usually try to end up with a strong fish.

Time and again I have lifted a fish out on to that little island, knocked him on the head and then have had to sit quietly a few minutes to calm my excitement and still the trembling of my hands. And all because of the intensity of ten or fifteen minutes with a little fish three or four pounds at the end of the line; it seems hard to believe and I always tell myself that I should be getting used to it, I should be able to take it more calmly. Yet I never do.

The typical pattern of a fresh steelhead's fight in the pool starts with a very fast run, straight from the strike, downstream and across to somewhere near the big rock on the far side. I touch nothing, just hold the rod and let him run and jump his best until the speed tapers off with anywhere from fifty to eighty yards of backing out. Then I check a little, very gently, and usually the fish comes back. If I move at all at that stage I go upstream, farther on to the bar, and a little across towards my own side. Sometimes, but not always, the run back is almost as fast as the run out. It is likely to stop about ten or twenty yards below the bar, where the water begins to shallow, and more often than not there is some slack line. The moment I tighten, the fish is away again, just as fast and almost as far as the first time. Again I let everything go, especially if the fish is jumping and curving his run upstream. As soon as the run checks I start moving across again, in earnest now, keeping well upstream still if the fish is big, working down a little if I think he is in the three- or four-pound class. I know he is tiring—he has to be. But I also know I must keep him tired.

This time he will come almost to the bar, but he will run

again when I tighten and he feels it over the shallows; perhaps twenty-five yards, but not nearly so fast and now under pressure, because I dare to finger the reel. By this time I have moved well across, almost to the line of the little island if I am lucky, but probably not that far. The fish will not come back from this run on his own. The rod must bring him. The bar has shallowed off so that many of the rocks are breaking water and the fish comes unwillingly among them. He will run again, ten yards, then five yards, then only two or three yards. I struggle to get him in some sort of sheltered water, behind a rock, behind the little island, but it is never easy. The end varies. Sometimes I risk the net and it is large enough. More often I strand his head on a rock and he lies briefly on his side for me to gill him; sometimes this takes two or three attempts and it is probably the most risky stage of the whole proceeding, though I cannot recall having lost one then.

That describes an average fight by one of these fish and an ideal plan of counteraction. Things don't always work out so smoothly; many a good fish shakes the fly in the first run; a few, very few, do so in their second or third runs; sometimes I misjudge a fish's strength, work down the bar too soon and have to follow him to the next pool; sometimes I have to work a strong fish away from the dangerous lip of the rapids by backing slowly and painfully upstream to lead him after me. There is plenty of variation. But none of them quits until the very end and by that time I am usually pretty exhausted myself, mainly through excitement and concentration.

One day in September of 1955 I hooked a particularly vigorous fish fairly well down the second main run. He

went off in the usual violent first run and broke it with
one of the loveliest jumps I have ever seen—end over end,
so high and fast that he seemed for a moment to float in
mid-air like a ballet dancer. A second later he was breaking
water under the far bank, below the big rock. He had a lot
of backing out—in fact I glanced down at the reel to see if
the splice at the end of the first hundred yards was showing—and he chose to fight where he was instead of coming
back. I tried to walk him upstream and had some success,
but he fought it all the way and it was a long while before
I could see my fly line again; and before I could bring the
splice to the rod-top he had made several more short runs,
all vigorous, twisting and dangerous. Everything held and
I finally managed to lead him down the bar, steer him headfirst into the net and lift him out. He hadn't a movement
left in him and both eyes were a glowing red, something
I have never noticed in a fish before. I am not anatomist
enough to know whether or not this could have been produced by a haemorrhage of some kind, but I feel certain
he had used his heart right up. He had fought for nearly
twenty minutes without a pause, yet he weighed only four
and a quarter pounds.

This fish impressed me as strongly as any of them, though
not more strongly than most. I remember him because of
his beautiful floating jump and the glowing eyes. As usual,
I tried to remember exactly where he had taken and exactly
how the fly had been floating, something I have trained myself to do fairly well under normal conditions. As usual
with one of these fish, I found I could not; the suddenness
and speed of the first run from the strike produces a brief
amnesia, which is fairly significant in itself.

It is hard to account for such quality of performance, but I can think of several factors that contribute to it. The fish are only a mile or two from salt water and have just come in—I do not think they lie much longer than two or three days in the Main Island Pool, if so long. The pool itself helps them, by its breadth and length, its swift current and its comparatively shallow water. The fact that nearly all of them rise to the fly in very shallow water makes for the immediate response to the prick of the hook—they know the bright sunlight over the shallows is no place for them. And I do my share to make the astonishing length of the runs by using no other pressure than the light check of the reel—though the fish really controls this too, since any additional pressure that can be applied is all too likely to break the leader or else to persuade the fish to keep on running right out of the pool.

I have been able to make a few comparisons with fish of other species hooked under almost identical circumstances in the same pool. Once I rose a bright ten-pound coho salmon to a floating fly in the main run. It never occurred to me he was anything but a steelhead and I was astonished when his first run took only ten or fifteen yards of line, then came to a dead stop. Rather nervously I put on pressure and brought him back almost to my feet. That seemed to convince him something was wrong. He jumped clear out, up to eye level it seemed, and was running when he hit the water again. The run went on and on, right down to the rock at the tail of the pool and beyond, but it was in spurts, now fast, now slow, rather than a continuous burst of speed.

I knew from the moment of his jump that the fish was a

coho, though I would not let myself believe it because I had never heard of any Pacific salmon being taken on a floating fly. So I wanted him very badly and did not take chances. He came back slowly and I felt sure he was tiring. At the edge of the shallow he made another jump, clear out, but a tiring jump. I saw I could work him and make him roll and flash with side strain, so I led him down the bar. Near the little island he attempted a rather weak run which I turned easily—something I probably should not have dared try with a steelhead. Then I stranded him on some rocks and gilled him without trouble. As soon as I had him on the island I made anal fin ray and gill-raker and caeca counts to guard against any later doubts about the identification. There were thirteen rays in the anal fin, twenty-two gill-rakers and around sixty-five pyloric caeca.

There was nothing wrong with the performance of this coho. His jumps were splendid, his run magnificent and he did a good deal more body twisting and head shaking than the steelheads; I had to discard the leader before I started fishing again because it was so badly twisted up. But he had none of the suddenness of the steelheads, nor the sustained speed, nor the stamina that keeps them strong to the very end.

I have also hooked tyee salmon of thirty, forty, perhaps even fifty pounds on the shallows close under the bar, using the five-ounce rod, a No. 6 wet fly and 0x or 1x leader. They usually start rather slowly, then run with great speed and power a very long way. If they choose to sulk there is not much to be done but break off the engagement. But if they continue to fight it is possible to work them in, steer them down inside the rocks and tail them in the lower pool.

This takes at least an hour and is an exhausting business; but it has nothing like the wild excitement of ten or fifteen minutes with a four-pound steelhead, and the exhaustion is physical rather than emotional.

Winter steelhead are usually a lot heavier and at their freshest they also can move with lightning speed and power the moment they feel the hook; but I am generally using a heavier leader so I put on some control almost from the start and do not get the same sense of uncontrollable speed. In the middle stages their performance slows appreciably and in spite of the power from their additional size and strength they are rarely so dangerous in the closing stages. This is probably due partly to the much colder water of wintertime, partly to the maturity of the fish, which are several months closer to spawning than the summer fish of August and September.

Summer steelhead I have caught on the dry fly in smaller streams at some distance from salt water are very much less spectacular. They rise more faithfully and are much easier to hook; the small pools limit their first few runs and even when they finally turn down and run out it is often possible to follow them down without yielding any backing at all. But it generally takes longer to beach them precisely because they haven't had either the will or the opportunity to run the fight out of themselves. One puts in some anxious minutes, especially when they are on a short line, but patience and pressure will get them in the end.

If I have made my Campbell summer steelheads sound like something unusual, it is because I honestly believe they are. There are not many of them, hardly enough to fish for; they are not so much a run as a few stragglers passing through, with perhaps one brief peak early in September. If I account for ten or a dozen in a season, I am doing very well. But I strongly suspect they are building themselves into a real run. If, as I hope, the increased summer flow of the river is speeding up this process, they will more than compensate for the disappearance of the harvest cutthroats. But I shall go on looking for the cutthroats. Even with a better fish in the river, it is hard to forget those brilliant August days with a small fly searching the smooth flow at the tail of the old Canyon Pool.

6. *The Dry Fly and Very Fast Water*

THERE ARE MANY OTHER STREAMS ON THE Pacific slope much like the Campbell, but with far better runs of summer steelhead. There isn't the least doubt that a floating fly will work on them just as well as it does on the Campbell, which means that it will get many more rises and probably kill more fish under most conditions than any sunk-fly technique. I am certain, too, that it will outfish spinners and lures and even bait anywhere except in the deep pools or in high water.

I realize this may sound like an extravagant claim, but I have had chances to make a few brief tests on other streams; these have convinced me that when a summer steelhead is lying in water of fast to moderate flow, not over four or five feet deep, he can be persuaded to come up to a big dry fly practically every time, provided he is approached with reasonable care and caution and cast to with reasonable skill.

I learned to fish a dry fly for brown trout on an English chalkstream. Many North American writers before me have described variations of this original technique that fitted it better to the waters they knew, none more ably than George La Branche. I cannot hope to emulate them in this short chapter, but the peculiarities of Pacific Coast fish and the very fast water of Pacific Coast streams have forced me into a good many variations of method that I have not seen recorded elsewhere. My chapter heading is chosen with due humility, as a gesture of respect to La Branche, who consciously developed new methods instead of merely being forced into them.

I have already described the suitable tackle. A light single-handed rod is pretty well essential if wrist and arm are not to be worn out by hours of searching and false casting and I have found a rod of eight feet, weighing four ounces, with a fairly stiff action, very comfortable to use. Mine is made of heat-treated cane by C. M. Gatley of Vancouver. It handles an HCH double taper line or an HCF or HDG forward taper with forty-five feet of belly ahead of the running line—enough for most dry-fly casts without the necessity of recovering several coils of light running line into the hand and the risk entailed in getting rid of them when a fish is hooked. A Hardy St. John reel is not too heavy for the rod and will carry a hundred yards of backing besides the fly line. The leader need not be lighter than 0x, though I prefer 1x with No. 8 flies and continue using a leader with No. 6's until it is cut back to 9/5 or .012″. I do not think the fly pattern matters too much, but it should be fairly dark, thick-bodied, with hair wings and tail to make it float well. The fish will take flies that sit well on good hackles, but I believe they will take more readily and more faithfully when the hackle is light and the body touches down on the surface film.

Wading is one of the first practical difficulties. One is normally working against the current, which can be hard and tiring. A wet fly can and should be left to rest in the

water as one moves between casts, but with a dry fly this
is not good since the fly will soak up water and lose its
floating qualities; so it must be kept in the air by false casting, which increases the difficulty. If the move is made
during the float of a cast it must be made blind, because it
is tempting fortune too much to look away from the fly
even for a second.

These difficulties are not too formidable in a stream with
a good gravel bottom—one can move safely without looking if necessary, and problems of balance are not so great
as to make false casting awkward. On slab rock with sharp
holes and other such dangerous places, one must look ahead
and the instinct of self-preservation makes certain that one
will, even at some risk of drowning the fly. In swift streams
with slippery bottoms of large round rocks, like the Campbell, only practice helps, but that helps a lot. I used to think
this half-blind wading an almost insufferable chore; I still
find it infinitely more exacting physically than downstream
wading, but I go about it with a good deal of pleasure and
satisfaction and rarely slip or stumble.

The secret is in slow and careful movement and in feeling with the feet. I usually move while false casting, which
gives one at least a chance to glance down at the bottom.
I push the leading foot firmly but slowly against the current
and feel for solid footing. If there is an obstruction I feel
for a way over or around it without committing myself too
far. If there is no way without making the stride too long,
I am content to set the leading foot down and bring the
other foot up to it, then try again.

All this becomes instinctive with practice and one can
work up a bad stretch of water very smoothly. In a difficult

place, crossing an especially fast run or getting around an unusually large rock, I let the fly swing straight below me on a short line, hold the rod high and leave it there dragging lightly on the surface while I move. I also help myself with the aluminum wading-staff that has been hanging behind me on a shoulder strap through the easier moves.

Another practical problem is floating the fly in fast and broken water and keeping it floating well. Good hair wings and hair tail are just about essential and will outlast anything else I know of. Thickly tied hackles of high quality are also excellent, but I am convinced that on most days I miss a higher proportion of rises to such flies than to flies with sparse, soft hackles. Some writers have suggested that this may be because the cushion of water formed against the neb of the rising fish pushes the fly away and so makes him miss; whatever the reason, it is a pity, because well-hackled flies certainly attract fish, they are easy to see and they float a long while. I use them, especially some very beautiful ones tied with clipped deer-hair bodies by Harry and Elsie Darbee of Roscoe, N. Y., but I am always ready to change promptly to a soft-hackled type if I miss a fish or two.

To float for any length of time a fly must be well greased and the silicones are best for this. If possible I soak my flies at home and give them time to dry out, then touch each one up again just before I start fishing with it. In really bad water a solid grease of the kind generally used for lines lasts longest. Lines themselves are no longer so much of a problem now that nearly every maker is turning out "bubble" or "hollow core" or some other type of permanent floater. I have one, but do not like it much because the front end of the taper is very heavy, so I generally find myself using a modern synthetic line, which is hardest of all to float but does surprisingly well if it is thoroughly greased. If it starts to give trouble one can easily wipe it with a dry rag, give it a few moments in the summer sun and grease it again.

I cannot convince myself that the dressing of the fly matters nearly so much as its size and form. A few of the fish I catch, both cutthroats and smaller steelheads, are feeding hard and when this is so their stomachs are practically always crammed with either sedge larvae or snails, without a sign of a winged creature to account for the surface rise; in other words, they are feeding on bottom and selectively and they come up from this serious business to the floating fly simply because it looks like an attractive and easily captured variation. This suggests a reason for the success of flies of large size that have either bulky bodies or bodies that rest on the surface film.

The majority of steelheads I catch of three pounds and up either have nothing at all in their stomachs or signs of very casual activity—a bee or two, a yellow jacket, a deer fly, occasionally a large sedge, sometimes a winged dragon-fly. They also have been attracted from the quiet business of absorbing oxygen and resting by the chance drift or float of something too tempting and conveniently placed to resist. These chance feeders seem to me to hint pretty plainly at the sort of fly dressing most likely to be effective. Bee, yellow jacket and deer fly are all somewhat similar in color and all seem to be taken with surprising frequency. So I prefer a fly with a dark-brown and yellow body, tied with light-brown hair wings and tail and a brown hackle. I very much doubt if any other pattern is necessary except

possibly to convince a fish that has already been stung by
the brown and yellow one. On a river with sparse hatches
of really large mayflies I should be tempted to try a big
spider if the fish came short to my usual offerings, but I
have not yet run into this.

Short casts, not over fifty feet and preferably nearer
thirty, are much the best if the water can be covered by
them, and there is not the slightest risk of disturbing fish
at even the lesser distance in rough and broken water when
working up from downstream. A long drift is essential because of the follow-back rises that are so common. This
means that the normal point of recovery would be approximately when the fly is nearest the rod-top in its travel
downstream, a silly place to recover because of the difficulty of picking up and the extra work of putting out the
line again. I simply let the fly go on past me, slipping out
the recovered line as it goes until only a coil or two is left
in my hand, then the fly sweeps round and rides the surface of the water directly below me. From there, watching
to make sure no fish is planning to grab it at the wrong
moment, I simply sweep it forward into the air, make my
false casts to shake the water off line and fly, and drop the
fly into its next drift.

In a cast that is made more across than upstream, the
long float is still important. This means drag unless something is done. As soon as a belly of line begins to show I
loop it upstream in a mend, usually giving the fly a slight,
intentional hop as I do so, then letting it float smoothly by
lowering the rod-top until the downstream loop begins to
form again. This hop of the fly is a deliberate use of drag
and I have known it stir up more than one unwilling fish.

It is fun to do and often can be repeated several times in the length of a drift.

The end of this drift is much like the end of the other—the fly is allowed to swing across, directly downstream, then lifted in a simple forward cast. I have stressed that it rides the surface in this movement. If it is dragged under each time it will soon pick up water and lose its float. For this reason, and also because it helps in controlling deliberate drag, I prefer a floating leader. I do not believe for a moment that it disturbs the fish in fast and broken water and a fly will keep its floating qualities at least as long again if the leader stays on top. If I expect to come to smoother water where a sinking leader is necessary, I carry a small sample tube of toothpaste in my fishing vest and rub a little along the leader to take the grease off.

One other difficulty in many streams, and especially in the Campbell, is that small fish, usually steelhead, parr or smolts, are often lying in exactly the same type of water as larger fish, sometimes within a few feet of them. These little fish rise swiftly and accurately and nearly always take the fly down. It is fairly easy to judge such rises for what they are and withhold any tightening of the line; nine times out of ten the fly will come freely away and, after a few false casts, be none the worst for being dragged under. I get rid of some hundreds of little fish in this way every season and rarely hook one. The little fish rises are splashy and unsubstantial; the big fish nearly always makes a noticeable swirl or surge, even if he is not himself visible. It is true that both large and small fish can, and do at times, rise with the tidiest dimple in the fastest water, but even then I believe there is a subtle but detectable difference in the rise form and one has plenty of time for a second thought about it because a strike that would hook the small fish would be much too fast for the big fish. I don't think I have ever been wrong about this, but I sometimes wonder if, in some afterlife, the devil will parade before me in endless procession all the big fish that have sucked down my flies and been allowed to spit them out without the slightest move on my part.

In searching summer steelhead streams my experience has been that the very best places are the narrow runs—narrow runs along the sides of pools, narrow runs between rocks and especially the narrow runs at the heads of the pools, some of which are very shallow. A fish waiting in such a place will nearly always rise to the first fly put over him. But if he misses it, especially on a downstream turn or a follow-back, he probably will not come again for the simple reason that he has startled himself and continued his movement to the safety of deeper water. The best thing then is to come back again in fifteen minutes or half an hour, when he will probably be back in position.

In searching water for steelheads, it is important to remember that they are migratory fish and almost certainly not feeding. Many places that are perfect lies for feeding trout are not steelhead lies at all. I do not think it is wise to make repeated casts over a known lie unless one is very sure a fish is holding there. If he is there he will probably rise or show the first time the fly is floated accurately to him, and it is more important to go on searching other water because the fish, especially if they are traveling, are often in unexpected places. On the other hand I think it is very important to search a run of any width with a suc-

cession of drifts, each a foot or so over from the last, because the fish will not always come to a fly unless it is
directly over them.

Striking the fish is a matter of enormous difficulty or
pure luck, especially in very fast water. In a run of easy
current it is simple enough; the rise is very slow, very
dignified and very faithful. One simply gives the fish lots
of time to start back down with the fly, then tightens on
him.

In very fast water the variety of rises can be almost infinite. Occasionally one gets a perfect head and tail rise,
surprisingly deliberate in spite of the speed of the current,
and again it is simply a matter of tightening as the fish goes
down. Nearly always the results are explosive and spectacular, though I have known the fly to come back without
the slightest feeling of resistance. This is usually the rise of
a big fish, over five pounds, perhaps over ten pounds.

But in very fast water the big fish will sometimes swirl
or splash or follow, especially to a dragging fly, and the
smaller fish, the two- and three- and four-pounders will
do it more often than not. These fish are the true grilse of
the steelhead runs—that is, they are both males and females
running up to spawn after only one year of sea feeding,
as do Atlantic salmon grilse. Out of the water they are
very handsome, mature, even noble-looking creatures, especially if one thinks of them as trout; in the water they are
wild, crazy, reckless and completely unpredictable. And
in the Campbell, at least at the present stage of the run's
development, they seem to be more abundant than the
regular four-year-olds, which are returning after two
years' sea feeding.

Normally when fish rise wildly and are hard to hook, one suspects the fly pattern. I have tried large flies and small, high-riding flies and low-riding flies, hard hackles and soft, bright patterns and dull ones, but have yet to find a fly that will hook these fish dependably or produce a more consistent foim of rise. A darkish fly, low-riding on soft hackles dressed on a No. 6 or No. 8 hook, does as well as anything I can find and I am now pretty well satisfied that the answer is not in the fly.

One thinks next of one's own performance—the strike to the rise, the tightening of the line that sets or should set the hook. I have tried just about all the variations of strike I can think of, including not striking at all in the hope that the drag of the line will be enough to set the hook. The best bet is just what one would think it should be—a slow easy tightening into the fish as he goes down with the fly; but even this gives a very low percentage of fish hooked, probably not one in three of the really fast rises. And there are times when it is obviously out of the question; when a fish follows back or swirls or does both directly towards the rod, and keeps coming in the same direction, about the only chance is to pick up slack as fast as possible and raise the rod as high as possible and hope that somehow the hook will set itself. It very rarely does.

The swirling rise has bothered me particularly. I have noticed quite often with small fish of a pound or so, which are always feeding, that the fast water swirl very often misses the fly completely and is followed by a very quiet approach from below and a gentle, honest take. This is easy to observe with small fish, because the disturbance of their swirl is not great and the fly, more often than not, is left floating. But with larger fish this swirl is always heavy enough to drown the fly and obscure it completely. One simply does not know whether or not the fish has it, so there is really nothing to do but tighten at the appropriate time and hope for the best. Sometimes he has it, sometimes he does not. A fish that swirls away from the rod will be hooked by tightening at least as often as not, so the swirling rises are by no means always mere attempts to drown the fly. If the fish has dragged it down with his swirl and is intending to circle back and take it, it would be nice to wait for him. But unless the fly is visible, either above or below the surface, it is a better gamble to tighten than to wait.

I think the reason for the high percentage of missed rises is not in the fly pattern nor usually in the fisherman's reaction to the rise, but in the wild, quick nature of the fish themselves and in the speed of the water, combined with the fact that the fish is not really feeding and that he rises always from the bottom. Still another factor may be in the type of insects most commonly found in these fish; dragonflies, bees, yellow jackets and hornets can all bite or sting back and it may be that fish take them rather lightly at first, let them go quickly, then turn at them again. In other words the trouble is not that the fisherman is missing fish he should hook, but that the fish themselves are often missing the fly completely or taking it very lightly.

This wouldn't matter so much if they would come a second time, but usually they will not, even when one has felt no slightest resistance to the strike. Changing the fly does not seem to help, but occasionally five or six casts to approximately the same spot with the same fly will bring a fish back. If he does not come in half-a-dozen casts he probably will not come in a dozen or in twenty. I believe this is because he has gone away from his rise into deep water and does not even see the fly again, rather than because he is afraid or suspicious of it. The best thing is to fish on and forget him after half-a-dozen drifts. But in an hour or less he will probably be back in position and ready to take again.

I have mentioned deliberate drag as a means of persuading reluctant fish to come up. Drag should never be used until a natural float has first been tried over the water, because drag, while it does bring up fish that might not otherwise move, far too often produces short rises. This does not apply to the very short drag or hop that can be produced by mending the line or a slight twitch of the rod-top, because the fly then settles back into natural drift before the fish takes. It is more an imitation of the movement of a live fly than drag. Nor does it apply to the skip and roll of a spider fly in the wind on a light leader. But it does most strongly apply to a fly dragged across the current or across an eddy into the current, and it applies also to the fly skipped upstream against the current wavelets.

The last is a very deadly trick at times, and it is readily used in very fast water. One simply fishes up a run in the normal way then, instead of passing on, works in very close to the head of the run. From there make a short cast on a slack line across the current, let the fly take its drift and swing around. When it is directly below, recover it gently so that it skips from the crest of one wave to the next, for about ten feet. Then let it drop back in a natural drift to the end of the line. This can be repeated again and again and in many variations until the whole run is covered, though fish are more likely to take where the run drops off into deeper water than anywhere else. Usually they take on the drift back, with a sharp swirl from one side or the other so that the chance of hooking them is good. But sometimes they boil up from directly behind the bouncing fly or even jump right out at it. This is very exciting, especially when a nine- or ten-pounder is suddenly out in the sunlight from nowhere and only twenty or thirty feet from the rod-top; but it doesn't often hook a fish.

If I could find fish of the same kind as close to home in easier water, I don't think I should bother much with these wild and swiftly passing creatures of the Campbell. But the Campbell is my home stream and these fish are both difficult and exciting, so I haven't the slightest excuse for not doing my best to meet them on their own terms. Since the summer height of the river is likely to be very steady from now on at around 4000 cubic feet a second, the fish will go on being difficult and fishing for them will continue to be hard work. But I am hoping that the more stable flow will give me a better idea of exactly where to look for them, and that the run will continue to build in numbers as I believe it has done over the past ten years. And finally I hope I shall get smarter at the whole business and learn to rise and hook a lot more of them than I have in the past.

7. *The Canyon Again*

THE 1958 SEASON ON THE CAMPBELL WAS the most difficult of all. In late July the river was high, but not too high; I managed to get out occasionally and took a few nice fish of well over three pounds, as well as rising others. It looked like a good start to a wonderful year.

Then, towards the end of the month, another turbine was cut in at the main powerhouse and the river came up to a steady level of 4000 cubic feet a second or more. At first I expected it would make little difference. It would be harder to work up against the current, of course, and some of the old favorite lies might be too fast to hold fish well. If so, it seemed probable that other lies in slightly easier water might come into use. I promised myself to search the edges of the runs with extra care, to remember high water lies where I had taken fish and, above all, to study the water closely for anything that might suggest a new holding place—a new glide beyond a fast run, narrow runs close against the bank, the reunion of currents behind big rocks, all the spots one would be likely to search if trying the river for the first time.

In this performance I think I was fairly faithful, as were others who fished with me. I conscientiously worked over places I have not fished for twenty years, and which have never given me a fish. I struggled upstream along the edges of the rapids, and gave the fly a chance in every place where the current smoothed or slowed. And I fished all

the familiar lies as thoroughly and regularly as I ever had.
It was a labor of love because I was constantly expecting
some fine new discovery. And I made some new discov-
eries, none of them the ones I had expected and hoped for.

The old lies still held fish, but they were little fish, running from twelve to seventeen inches, instead of the fish
of eighteen inches and over I was looking for. Occasionally a really good fish flashed at the fly just where he was
supposed to be, but they were few and not a single one
was properly hooked, though I can still remember two or
three head and tail rises at the very start of the float that
seemed completely honest, until I tightened and felt nothing at all. Once I tightened on a fish of seven or eight
pounds that had swirled away from me in the main run of
the Island Pool, felt him solidly, then had the fly come
away before he had taken more than a coil or two of line
from my hand.

None of this seemed too surprising. After all, the fish
never had been abundant. With the faster and deeper water
it seemed natural enough they should be harder to find and
probably harder to rise; they were always hard to hook,
and if a higher percentage than ever before was missing
the fly altogether, that also could be explained by the
faster water. But August went on into September and
though I fished regularly I still hooked nothing at all over
sixteen or seventeen inches and the occasional rises from
larger fish became fewer instead of more numerous. Perhaps the run had failed, perhaps the higher water had somehow changed its pattern. I puzzled over it and wracked my
brain for a theory worth testing, but got nowhere. The
fishing I had learned to expect and count on during the
previous eight or ten years simply was no longer there.

In its place was something else—the smaller fish. Most of them were rainbows, bright silver and fresh from the sea, usually maturing to spawn though not within several months of doing so. A few were cutthroats, small dark fish often in very poor condition—fish such as I had never seen in the Campbell before. Two of the poorest were like snakes, a little over thirteen inches long and weighing less than four ounces; neither had spawned and both were carrying sea lice. The summer was an unusually dry one and most of the smaller streams and creeks had very little water, so it seemed just possible that these little fish had been attracted by the heavy flow of fresh water from the Campbell. But if so, why hadn't some of their larger and better-conditioned brothers and sisters come along with them? It all remained a puzzle—the sort of puzzle one struggles with for a while, then leaves to be clarified by the experience of succeeding seasons.

I was inclined to do the same with the puzzle of my missing steelhead run. Then, towards the end of September, I thought again of those six turbines throwing out water into the surge pool. The two newest turbines were on the outside, towards the center of the river. The stream from them would be farther over towards the north bank— far enough, perhaps, to make some flow once more over the fantail of the Canyon Pool, where the harvest cutthroats had rested and risen in the years before the dam. It seemed possible that a few of them might be resting there again, even though it was late in the season; and rather more than possible that my missing steelheads might also have passed on to the shelter of the big pool.

In the days before the dam it was a pleasant walk up the

north bank of the river to the pool. There was an easy-going trail among the ferns under the big maples and hem-locks, wandering past the Island Pools, gently climbing the sidehill above the long rapid by the Upper Island, easing down again to the flat rock bench at the mouth of the canyon. Loggers went along part of the way some twenty years ago and did their share of damage; but at least they took out their logs without smashing everything down and the debris they left has mostly rotted away. A more heed-less and wasteful breed has followed them—the construc-tion men.

Along the Main Island Pool, half-a-dozen big trees have been felled into the river and secured to their stumps by heavy cables—for what reason I cannot guess, unless it was to protect the logging bridge that was thrown across the head of the Sandy Pool and used for a single season. On the sidehill above the Upper Island there is a chaos of random destruction—the power line right-of-way. Great trees have been felled in every direction, uphill, downhill and across. Some have driven their heavy heads straight down into the riverbed and these too have been securely cabled in case some kindly freshet should come to clear away some of the mess. Fifty years will not rot those trees away, four hundred years wouldn't put them back. And all this devastation is within the boundaries of a provincial park.

. I had seen it all before, of course, but that didn't make it any better and I arrived at the pool breathing fire and uttering unprintable words to reduce the pressure within. The final insult is a gigantic hemlock well beyond the power lines, felled headfirst down the hill to shatter its top against the river bottom just below the pool and make a perfect trap for any good fish that chooses to run out in a hurry.

The canyon itself and the body of the pool was still dead water. A few humpbacks broke water there, pieces of bark and other flotsam drifted aimlessly. A confused or sun-loving bat hunted among them. But the outside turbines were throwing water and, I thought, some of it was spreading over the old holding bottom, choppy and broken instead of glass-smooth, but drawing pleasantly.

I waded in at the tail, uncomfortably deep and stumbling around among the big rocks. It was an awkward backhand cast and the sun was so squarely in my eyes that I could only see the fly as it pitched and follow its float by dodging my head. A small fish rose. I let him shake it, recovered and cast again. There was another rise and just for a moment, in the glare of the sun, I thought it small again. But there was a surge from this rise and I recognized it just in time to tighten smoothly into a good fish. He ran hard upstream, jumped nobly and came back, then ran again. The big tree below had me thoroughly scared and when he came back the second time I thought he would run past it. A belly of slack line turned him, on the wrong side of the big rock. He came up past it and from there I manhandled him into quieter, though still not quiet, water near the bank. Three or four minutes later I got the net under and lifted him— or rather her—out; a perfect female steelhead of just over three pounds, bright and clean with tiny ovaries and an empty stomach.

After that I missed a fish or two, never quite sure whether they were large or small because of the dazzling sun. Then I had another, a twin of the first though a fraction under three pounds. Then a sixteen-inch cutthroat, fat and bright, a male with a good-sized bullhead in his stomach. All these fish had risen in a little triangle of water, where the throw of the run from the outside turbine spread against the dead water of the canyon and drew down over the tail of the pool. When I threw beyond it, into the run, no good fish rose at my fly. And there were no good fish in the slack edge against the dead water.

With the rise of the cutthroat I had pretty well covered the magic triangle, so I came out of the water and went up to the flat rock bench at the head of the pool. There I put on a wet fly, threw it across the dead water and worked it back several times to see if anything would follow. There was nothing, though in the old days of flow through the canyon every cast would have drawn half-a-dozen yearling steelheads. I worked back down again with the wet fly, reaching over to the outside run from the surge pool and easing it back into the productive triangle, but nothing came to it except small fish. So I changed back to the dry fly, faced into the sun again, made a cast and was into a good fish immediately. That one shook the hook somewhere below the big rock. The next one I missed. The third, another steelhead grilse exactly like the first two, came into the net and finished my day.

It was a nice catch from a few yards of water, fully up to the standards of the old Canyon Pool, though the fish were steelheads and not cutthroats. I felt I had come on at least part of the answer to my poor season—the fish were passing up the fast water runs of the Island Pools to find the deep water of the Canyon Pool again.

Whether or not that is the end of the story, it is hard to tell. I rather think not. As the river holds on at its new level the summer fish will find new lies in it, not merely in the canyon, but in all the pools. And the make-up of the runs themselves is still changing. The big cutthroats, it seems, have pretty well disappeared. A few good-sized steelheads, anywhere from five to fifteen pounds, are still running in—and their numbers may be increasing. The steelhead grilse, two- and three- and four-pounders, are surely holding their own and probably increasing. And then there are the little grilse, the fish that have been so suddenly abundant this year, fish running from twelve to sixteen or seventeen inches. What they are and why they are, I don't pretend to guess. But from second spawners among these and the larger true grilse, surely it isn't too much to hope for an increase in the run of big fish. And from the increased flow of the river surely I can hope, too, for an increased survival from the spawnings of all three types.

As for the Canyon Pool or the Powerhouse Pool or whatever it should now be called, I am both glad and sorry to have rediscovered it. It is an awkward and unsatisfactory place to fish. I don't care for the blind windows of the powerhouse looking down on me as I fish, nor for the insult of the slashed-out right-of-way where the power line crosses the head of the Upper Island and climbs the hill below the pool. I don't care for the roar of the surge and the hum of generators in what was once a lovely silent place, nor for the stagnation of the canyon water. But I think I shall slowly come to terms with all these things and perhaps even learn an affection for them in the end. And since the fish are there again I am fully resolved to find ways to fish for them without awkwardness and ways to catch them with satisfaction.

PART FOUR

Poisson Bleu — The Flower of Fishes

1. *Standard-Bearer—Arctic*

T HE FIRST GRAYLING I CAUGHT WERE among the most difficult fish I have ever fished for. I was about sixteen at the time and the river was the Isla, a tributary of the Scottish Tay. I was visiting my friend, John Kinloch whose father, Sir George, was a grayling enthusiast.

For a sixteen-year-old, I was a fair dry-fly fisherman,

though probably not as good as I thought I was. But the Isla was a river quite unlike my little sparkling Frome at home; it was big and slow and usually rather deep. It had brown trout and occasional sea trout as well as grayling, but Sir George soon convinced me that these were easy and simple-minded fish beside the grayling. The grayling, he explained, is a very quick-sighted fish—as Pritt expresses it: "the gimlet eye of a mother-in-law is not more piercing than the optic of a grayling"—he is a difficult fish to rise because of this, a difficult fish to strike because of his small mouth and a difficult fish to play because his mouth is so soft. Sir George also explained to me how to recognize the quiet, sucking rise of a grayling, which generally leaves a few bubbles on the surface of smooth water. And I went on my way to see what I could do with the grayling of the Isla.

I caught brown trout, I caught a good big sea trout or two and I certainly rose several grayling. But I did not land one the first day, nor the second, nor the third, and by that time there was nothing in the world I wanted so much as to catch a fine big silvery grayling of the sort that Sir George brought home every day. I managed it in the end—that is, I successfully rose, hooked and landed a few fish of fair size—but I came away from the Isla with a very healthy respect for the grayling and all his arts.

From time to time thereafter I had chances to catch a few grayling on the Itchen and other south of England streams, and I found no reason to revise my opinion of them. They were, it seemed to me, just as difficult as well-educated brown trout; and while they did not fight so vigorously their soft mouths made careful and skillful handling highly important. These fish were the European grayling, *Thymallus thymallus*, silvery, graceful and attractive fish but not, as I recall it, very brilliantly colored.

More than twenty years passed between the netting of my last European grayling and the capture of my first Arctic grayling. During World War II, while serving in the Army, I was lent for some months to the Royal Canadian Mounted Police. In due course my duties took me into the far north and by good fortune I found myself fog-bound for several days at the mouth of the Coppermine River, in Coronation Gulf, on the Arctic Ocean. With a fine river close at hand, there was a fairly obvious duty to go fishing.

Through most of the war I carried with me a fly reel with an HCH line and plenty of backing, a few leaders and some flies, on the theory that where there are fish there is always a rod of some kind. Unfortunately on this occasion my kit bag had been stolen a few weeks earlier and the reel and line with it. I had some flies and a few leaders. The R.C.M.P. plane gave up from somewhere in its bowels a rusty steel telescopic rod and a length of cuttyhunk line; no reel. I plaited a sort of shooting head into the cuttyhunk, greased it well and wound the rest on to a piece of wood. Peter Natit, a charming Eskimo boy, was more than willing to guide me ten or twelve miles up the river to Bloody Falls, which is the best fishing place. But, he warned me, it was really too early. There would likely be nothing there but blue fish. Blue fish, I knew, were grayling, and I assured him I wanted nothing better.

Apart from the mosquitoes, which can be pretty terrible, no country in the world is more exciting and satisfying than the Arctic tundra in summertime. The endless rolling miles of spongy moss and knee-high willow are full of un-expected plants and flowers. Little lakes and good big streams are everywhere. It is a wild untouched land where sight of wolf or cariboo or barren lands bear may never be far away. There is the infinite day of high summer to mark it a place apart, even though the flowers bloom and mosquitoes hum; and over it all is the sense of the fierce, harsh winter that is never far away. In the signs of wind erosion, in the dwarfed plants, in the salt-water ice floes, in the cold of fog or the strong heat of the brief sun, in the up-turned sleds and the tethered lines of dogs and even in the talk and laughter of the Eskimos, is the feeling that summer is only a tiny, unreal interlude. On either side of it, at only a little distance, are the realities of ice and wind-swept snow, the zest of fall journeys, followed by the long night in which few creatures move.

I admit I enjoy these feelings and foster them, and Peter seemed to share them as we made our way up the ten or twelve miles of river to Bloody Falls. He talked eagerly of hunting and fishing and of the winter journeys by dog sled. He watched constantly for wolves and once took a shot at one, briefly silhouetted on a high cut-bank of the river two or three hundred yards away. We landed, of course, climbed the bluffs, found tracks, but no other sign of wolf.

I knew the story of the massacre at Bloody Falls, the meeting of Indian and Eskimo, the promise of friendship, the sudden fear-inspired treachery of the night attack. But I was not prepared for the falls themselves, which are not true falls but a tremendous gush of water through a narrow gut, which sends a great curling furrow, a long foaming wave six or eight feet high, to roll over and fold under like earth from a giant plowshare. It was magnificent and far more impressive than any single cascade of water over a rock face. To a canoeman it seemed the earth's supreme rapid, the ultimate challenge, and I was glad there were no other canoemen and no canoes around, though Peter told me that at least one young Eskimo had run it—whether successfully or not, I cannot now remember.

But I had better get to the grayling. On the way upriver I had stopped occasionally to try my awkward tackle in what looked to be promising places, though Peter assured me they promised very little—the place, he said, was the falls. Now, looking at them, I wondered where. We were standing on a wide rock bench on the right bank, with that gigantic fold of water tearing head high past us not fifty feet away. But there were eddies of almost smooth water close against the rock. Peter pointed to them; I watched one briefly and wondered why anything would bother to shelter in such a tiny pocket. Then, standing well back on the rock, I swung the rod in two or three jerky false casts and let my brown and white bi-visible flop forward into the quiet water.

Peter was a very polite and tolerant young man, which is something I have learned to expect of guides in out-of-the-way places. But his politeness and tolerance held no slightest hint of skepticism for my strange tackle or my little brown and white fly. He was more than open-minded; he was enthusiastic about both and we were equal partners in them exactly as we had been when he asked me to estimate the range of the wolf he had fired at. His faith and

enthusiasm were rewarded before the fly had bobbed for
five seconds on the surface of the water. A big grayling
came up in a head and tail rise, took the fly down and was
securely hooked.

The fish fought in short downward runs within the narrow limits of the pocket. It was blue, a changing turquoise
blue that showed in one moment and was lost in the next.
When we got her on to the rocks the blue showed vividly
along her back and the huge dorsal fin amazed me not only
by its size—I was too many years from the European fish
to appreciate the full significance of *Thymallus signifer*,
the Standard-Bearer—and its scarlet border, but by the
iridescent turquoise of its heavy spots. In the Arctic fog,
beside the mighty rush of the falls, with Peter's delight no
less than my own, the whole fish had a special beauty that
has never faded in my memory; but there are degrees of
vividness even in such a thing as this, and it was the splen-
dor of the blues that dazzled my mind's eye in its many
moments of recall during the next several years.

The Coppermine grayling were almost shamefully easy
to catch. There were one or two in every likely pocket
along the edge of the falls and soon Peter, not I, was catching them, handling the rod with his people's natural skill,
laughing and shouting with unrestrained delight at each
rise and strike and run. The fish were of good size, the
general run a little over seventeen inches long, but some
eighteen and nineteen inches. One or two of the pockets
had smaller fish which we returned, but where streamlets
overflowing from the rush of the falls ran through crevices
in the rock bench we found more good fish. These had less
color because they had not spawned that year, but when
turned in the light their sheen was even more vivid, faintly

echoing the turquoise over the whole silvery body surface.

After awhile we had had enough fishing, so turned up over the tundra to make a pot of tea in the priests' cabin, where the Oblate father stayed when he came to the fishing grounds with the Eskimos. From there we walked on, looking for wolves, birds, anything that would show itself. In the dripping fog, in the middle of the nesting season, I suppose it was not really a day for seeing things and we saw very little—a raven, a pair of American pipits, a few sandpipers, perhaps other birds I do not remember, and one or two mice—but it didn't seem to matter very much; simply to walk the springy moss, cross the wet gullies and feel the fog-shrouded space about us was enough.

In the end we came back to the falls and tried the grayling again. It was long after midnight when we got back to the settlement, but that did not matter either for daylight was still strong, everyone was up and about and we cooked a great feast of grayling. After that we talked until the clock said we should be starting a new day, then went to bed for an hour or two because it seemed wrong not to sleep at all.

The Coppermine grayling were one of my very few wartime fishing experiences—with a non-combatant's job, an infantryman's heart and a puritan conscience one has little inclination to make opportunities and even a certain reluctance to take advantage of them when they turn up. Several times I stopped a car along the Alaska Highway to watch grayling rising in the Teslin or the Liard or some other stream, but it was more than ten years before I fished for them again. In all that time the memory of the shape and grace and color of the Coppermine fish was so strongly with me that I began to be afraid I should not find it again.

2. *Standard-Bearer—by the Roadside*

Accoding to Jordan there are, or were, three North American graylings, the Arctic, the Michigan and the Montana, which he distinguished as *Thymallus signifer, T. tricolor* and *T. montanus.* Frank Forester, writing years earlier, seems to have known only of the Arctic grayling, and that at second-hand through Richardson, who named it from a specimen taken on the fly by Midshipman Back in the Winter River, near old Fort Enterprise in the Northwest Territories. Francesca LaMonte, a much more recent authority, recognizes only the Arctic grayling and the American grayling. She rates the American grayling as only subspecifically different from the Arctic, *T. signifer tricolor*, and includes both the Michigan and the Montana graylings in the term, since they are not scientifically separable.

I am not sure the term "American Grayling" is satisfactory; after all, the Arctic grayling is also an American grayling. Both "Michigan grayling" and "Montana grayling" are terms long used by anglers and they have important values of association. I have seen a report that the Michigan grayling stock is extinct; Jordan remarked in 1902 that it was already seriously depleted and that no great success had even been attained with artificial propagation. Artificial propagation of the Montana grayling, on the other hand, had already proved highly successful. I am not too clear about what has happened since that time, but the Montana grayling is becoming something of a favorite for the artificial stocking of clear, cold mountain streams, and some have already been planted in eastern British Columbia. I have every intention of making a special effort to catch some at the first good opportunity, preferably in their native domain at the headwaters of the Missouri. While I do not expect the Tricolor Standard-Bearer to exceed the beauty of the Standard-Bearer himself, I am prepared to find a very handsome fish and perhaps some altogether new delight of color.

Not too long ago, the Arctic grayling was a fairly inaccessible fish—true to his name, he frequents only the streams and lakes of the Arctic watershed. But with roads pushing steadily northward in almost every part of Canada since the war, the Arctic grayling is now within any fisherman's reach. And, quite apart from his beauty, he is well worth any fisherman's while. Unlike trout, grayling tend to school in considerable numbers. The mature fish are likely to be very even in size—within an inch or two of length, that is—in any given locality. They seem to love broad, fast runs of water that vary from three to six feet in depth. And they feed primarily on small insects, so they are ideal fish for the fly-fisherman—under most circumstances for the dry-fly fisherman. They do not fight as well as trout, but they are quite active enough to be interesting on very small flies and light gear. The only real fault I can find with them is that they are altogether too easy to catch, but that may very well correct itself in time, as more and more fishermen contribute to their education.

Two or three years ago my son Alan and I were in North Central British Columbia. Alan was anxious to broaden his range of fishing achievement by adding some new fish to his list. We had to go into Fort St. James, which is less than fifty miles from the divide between Arctic and Pacific watersheds, so I promised him grayling and whitefish in such streams as the Nation, the Manson and the Germansen, which are tributary to the Parsnip and Finlay rivers above the junction that makes the Peace.

Unfortunately this was not primarily a fishing trip—there was other work to be done. We struggled into Fort St. James with one tire flat and two others losing air fast. No garages were open and by the next morning the weather had changed to heavy rain.

A change of plan was inevitable if I was to complete the research work I had laid out for myself and it quite plainly meant we had better miss out the Nation and the other streams. "Don't worry, though," I said. "We've got to go into Fort McLeod and I know the Pack River, just beyond there, has grayling in it. Probably whitefish too."

We went back to Prince George, bargained for a couple of fairly good used tires and took the John Hart Highway north to Fort McLeod. The next morning I was asking questions about the Pack River grayling.

"No use now. They don't seem to stay in the river much after June."

It was mid-August.

"What about the Parsnip?" I asked. The road crossed it about fifteen miles farther on.

"Never heard of anybody fishing for them there."

"They'd have to be there, though," I said.

"Might be some—if you could find them."

We drove on to the highway bridge over the Parsnip. It is a wide, swift, shallow river, as I knew from Alexander Mackenzie's hundred-and-fifty-year-old description. But it was also much lower and clearer than I had dared hope. Above the highway bridge the broad river was split by several islands and that seemed the best place to begin the search.

Below the first island was a wide smooth flat along the right bank and fish were rising all through it.

"They look small," I told Alan. "But if we can catch one or two they'll tell us what to expect."

We caught one or two, after some difficulty in hooking them, and they were little silvery grayling about four inches long. The flat was only a nursery, but it was plain there were plenty of grayling in the Parsnip. All we had to do was find water where the adults lived and fed.

It was closer than I had dared hope. At the head of the island the water narrowed to a nice dancing run about a hundred feet wide. At the first float of the fly a fifteen-inch grayling showed prettily in a head and tail rise and was hooked. A few moments later we were admiring the bluish-purple sheen that glowed along his side as the pressure of the rod turned him off-balance in shallow water.

Where there is one grayling there will certainly be more, and this was water that could be readily fished without wading, so I left Alan to it and worked on upstream among the islands. I found another wide smooth flat, deeper than the first and dimpled everywhere with rises. The fish were grayling and whitefish, with a slight preponderance of the latter. I hooked a dozen or more, some of them over likely places in fairly deep water, but they were all small, around nine or ten inches, and I decided the flat must be a sort of intermediate school, between the nursery and the run Alan was fishing; I began to wonder what was the mature run of the stream. Would it be fish of the size Alan was probably catching or something larger?

It was easy to move about the river and I hunted fairly extensively, working upstream at first, then coming back down outside the islands. There were no wide fast runs of moderate, even depth—several times I thought I had found one, but each time found it too shallow. A dozen places looked like perfect holding spots for trout, but all were empty. I came round the last island and turned upstream again to join Alan. He was bringing a nice grayling into the beach as I came up to him.

"Well done," I said. "Want to keep him?"

He shook his head. "No. You can catch them one after another from here. But look what I've got. I kept them to show you. *Three* new kinds of fish."

And there they were—grayling, whitefish and Dolly Varden. "Haven't you caught a Dolly Varden before?" I asked.

"No," he said. "Three new fish in one day. That's something. And all standing in exactly the same place."

"All on dry fly?"

He nodded. "I kept it floating fine."

"Must be a record of some sort," I said. "Go on and catch some more. I know there are rainbows in the Pack and they might be down this far. Could be a sucker in there too, and heaven knows what all else. You might break your own record."

But the original record stood. There were plenty of grayling, all around the same fourteen- or fifteen-inch level and a few whitefish of about the same size, but no additional species.

The logical thing seemed to be to go back to the bridge, eat lunch and then try downstream. It was a gray and hazy sort of day, but the colors of the fish were showing up quite nicely and I hoped we might possibly get them with a camera. Besides there was still a possibility of much larger grayling. The Parsnip is a good big stream and well south for grayling water. It seemed to have plenty of feed and with a much longer growing season I felt it could reasonably be expected to do better than the eighteen- and nineteen-inch fish I had caught in the Coppermine, nearly a thousand miles farther north.

Below the bridge the river gathered itself into a good solid flow, varying in depth up to five or six feet and probably three or four hundred feet wide at its summer level. We fished down with wet fly, found a little pocket of grayling rather quickly, picked up two small Dolly Vardens and then, still not half a mile below the bridge, came upon grayling in abundance.

They were rising steadily in a wide run of fast, rippling water. Alan was enthusiastic about the idea of pictures and began at once to build a little pool at the edge of the river with a retaining wall of rocks, while I changed over to a dry fly.

Except that the fish rose so faithfully and freely, it was beautiful fishing. They were a little larger than those above

the bridge, fifteen or sixteen inches long. I had to wade
well out to reach them and the water they were in was
really fast, but they intercepted every fly unfailingly in
quick, graceful head and tail rises that showed their whole
bodies, perfectly controlled in the current. Hooked, they
ran quite well, even jumped occasionally, and they resisted
the approach to shallow water quite convincingly.

It was in this last stage that they were truly spectacular.
On even keel they seemed almost drab, clear olive-brown
shapes brightened only by the scarlet edge of the big
dorsal and the scarlet rays of spread pectorals. Then, in a
moment of struggle against the restraint, the whole fish
would be lighted with a glory of living blue sometimes
shaded to purple, sometimes violet, sometimes turquoise.
I delivered each one safely to Alan and soon he had six or
eight in the first pool and was building a second. I suggested we had enough. "No, no," he said. "Keep on. Get
all you can."

"Why don't you fish awhile? You could wade out far
enough."

"No, I'd rather watch them." There was no mistaking
that; he was absorbed, first by the multitude of fishes that
the river seemed willing to yield, then by the color and
form and movement of the fish themselves. Before long
the second pool had its quota and I stopped fishing. I had
used the opportunity to try a wide variety of patterns and
sizes of fly. Pattern did not seem to matter. In size I had
started out with No. 14's, which were hard to see in the
broken water—hard for me, that is, though not for the
grayling—and worked steadily up to a No. 8 Spruce fly.
The fish still came well to the larger flies, but were less

accurate. I missed one or two on No. 10's and at last two fish missed the No. 8 altogether, leaving it still floating after the rise. I hooked the next fairly and brought him in. The next went off downstream in a run that would have done credit to a two-pound rainbow and when he came in I saw the hook was set just under his vent.

I think that was the last one we took and we settled by the pools to study our catch. There was no light for pictures, but light enough to bring up the colors to the human eye. Alan said he had the fish already tamed, which seemed to be true—they were very tolerant of underwater handling and showed no signs of panic, though one or two found a hole in the wall of the first pool and took off before it could be blocked.

"When they spread their fins out," Alan said. "You can hardly push them over."

It was true. With their handsome pectorals spread against the bottom the fish were very solid in the water. It was almost impossible to turn them on their sides without gripping them and lifting them. "Why do you suppose that is?" he asked.

"I don't know," I said. "But it's probably a good part of the reason why they can rise so fast and accurately in fast water."

"Is the big dorsal fin the same?"

"I rather doubt it. I think it's more for display at spawning time. But it could help in keeping them squared away. These fish haven't got nearly such brightly colored fins as the Coppermine fish, but the body colors are better."

"Why is that?"

"Probably because they haven't spawned. If these spawn

next spring the dorsals will likely get much more red on them and brighter blue spots. The body colors will be more solid, less of a sheen."

The fish were quiet and patient in their little prisons, their graceful olive-brown bodies resting on the spread pectorals. It was nice to have caught them and watched them, nicer still to have them still alive.

"Shall we let them go?" Alan asked.

We broke the rock walls and let them find their own way out, watching their slow acceptance of the freedom of the river.

"It's been a good day," I said.

Alan watched the last fish swim slowly away.

"It sure has," he agreed.

3. *Standard-Bearer—*
Subarctic

A YEAR OR SO AGO THE GOVERNMENT OF Saskatchewan invited me to visit the province as guest speaker for Forest Conservation Week. At the end of it, the invitation added, "We can arrange to fly you into the north country for a few days' grayling fishing."

Here, quite plainly, was a summons to follow the Standard-Bearer which could not be disregarded. Towards the middle of May my wife, Ann, and I left the Pacific Coast for Saskatchewan. Forest Conservation Week was hard work and it was more nearly two weeks than one. But it was also a great deal of fun. Saskatchewan in springtime is as lovely a place to be as any on the face of the earth, and especially exciting for rainforest dwellers like ourselves. The great level spaces all about us, newly seeded black earth, green of springing wheat, dun of unturned stubble, freed the eyes and gave them new perspective, the enormous sky above was infinity realized and in the cloud shapes was past, present and future all at once.

I have heard old Northwest Mounted Policemen talk about the prairies as they were—a land one could ride across for days upon days without change; buffalo grass waving and rippling in the winds; the sudden flowers in springtime, bluffs of poplar and willow, potholes and sloughs and marshes sparkling in the sunlight and alive with waterbirds. A land to breathe in and grow in, they said. A land for the joyful and young in heart to rejoice in and remember.

It still is all these things. Where the buffalo grass is gone the wheat ripples no less bravely in the winds. The skies are no less wide and blue, the clouds are as white and high or as dark and storm-filled. The cities are lost and dwarfed a few miles from their outskirts, and they are few. The farm buildings shelter in their little belts of trees, scarcely noticeable in the reach of land and sky. And spring breaks as it always has, in a flood of freshness and of life renewed.

As we drove the long graveled miles from one little town to the next, there was always time to stop at some of the sloughs and marshes. Nowhere else is there such concentrated richness of life, or such vibrant life. Yellowheads and redwings endlessly chatter and sing in the reedy edges and flash their vivid jewels of head or wing in the sunlight. Shoveler, mallard, pintail, widgeon, bluewing and greenwing are there in all the glory of breeding plumage. Coots and grebes poke their way among the reeds. Willets and avocets wade the shallows. Gulls and swifts and terns dart and circle overhead. The marsh hawk hunts on long, slow wings. Scaups and ruddy ducks dive and dive again. Everything preens or displays or courts or swims or flies or wades or briefly hides and the whole marsh is a stir of color and life and sound and changing patterns of movement that never stops or slackens.

But all that is a long way from the grayling of the subarctic, though it was a worthy prelude to him and a natural progression towards him.

The official tour of the province ended at Prince Albert

on about the last day of May. Early the next morning, in a
driving rainstorm, we took off from the North Saskatchewan River and flew a hundred and fifty miles northward to
Lac la Ronge. From la Ronge, where the road ends in a
cluster of settlement at the lake edge—trading stores, government offices, freight canoes and tourist cabins side by
side and strangely intermingled—we took off again and flew
northwestward another two hundred miles. The country
had changed sharply from the sandy forested hills north of
Prince Albert, continuing almost to la Ronge, to the sparsely
treed gray rock of the Canadian shield. There was water
everywhere, water in lakes and ponds and potholes, in swift
rivers and in slower ones ox-bowed through muskeg, in
streams and streamlets and swamps. And for miles upon
endless miles there was more of the same—blue lakes and
green ones, occasional brown ones, some with floating ice
cakes, some still frozen, perhaps with the track of a winter
freight road still plain on the ice surface. Apart from this
last there was no sign of men; yet somewhere down there
men were, a very few men—fishermen, late trappers, early
prospectors.

Flying over it all I thought of grayling, great-finned turquoise-spotted grayling in the short reach of the Black Birch
River that joins Careen Lake to the Clearwater. I had never
been there before. The idea had come in a few telephoned
words from Wilf Churchman, the Deputy Minister, several
months ago. I had crossed salt water, flown over the Coast
Range and the Rockies and traveled slowly northward
through the length of a province while spring was coming
to the northland. Now I was flying again, straight as the
arrow of fate over two hundred miles of lakes and muskeg

and rock of the Canadian shield, to my meeting with them. They were dark shadows stirring under the break of the rapid below the still frozen lake, like other shadows stirring in the streams above and below the hundreds of other lakes we were passing over. Few other humans were within hundreds of miles of them and those few—Indian trappers and commercial fishermen—cared nothing for the great-finned grayling, only for jackfish, lake trout and whitefish. Only I, selecting this pinpoint of space in a million square miles, would disturb their peace. What did I want of them?

Not to kill them, certainly, nor to eat them, though I would probably do both these things. Not even to match my skill against their instincts, because I cheerfully assumed they would be rising freely, as Arctic grayling so frequently are, and present me no problems. Not for the excitement of setting light tackle against their strength and watermanship, for I had long ago learned to handle faster and stronger fish on lighter gear than they would make me use. Really it was only to see them and know them, and through them somehow to become more intimate with the land about the streams their presence graced.

These may not be exactly the thoughts expected of a normal fisherman, but to me they were intensely exciting and moving. They were with me as we circled over the raddled ice of Black Birch Lake, trying to judge whether Albert had left the cabin there to meet us at Careen. They were with me still as we tried to set down on the little ice-free bay by the quonset lodge on Careen Lake, with me as Sam McKnight swung the plane over the saddleback behind the lodge and put it down on the narrow waters of the grayling pool itself.

The grayling pool is a long wide reach of the Black Birch River, too long, too wide and too still to encourage fishing. But at the head of it the water from Careen Lake comes in over a strong rapid, almost a fall, a hundred yards wide and broken by two or three islands and several great rocks. Here, in the streamy water and close under the turbulence of the entering rapid, the grayling lie.

I expected them to be easy and fished confidently up the nearest run with a No. 14 dry fly. Nothing moved to it. At the head of the run the light was favorable and I looked back into the water. At first I could see nothing, then the shadowy shape of a cruising fish, then another and another. I couldn't be sure whether or not they were grayling, but they certainly looked as though they could be taken. Most of them were three or four feet down or deeper, but occasionally one came up to roll, or perhaps rise, at the surface. I let my No. 14 fly sink and drift down among them like a nymph. Something took lightly, was briefly hooked and let go. Then I hooked a whitefish, a strong broad-sided creature of over three pounds; and finally a grayling of seventeen inches.

But I knew then that I had come upon Arctic grayling in a different mood and it wasn't going to be entirely easy. We took several grayling on that first afternoon and a number of whitefish too. But even Norm Ferrier, that skillful northern fly-fisherman from the University at Saskatoon, was puzzled. Albert, the fine Cree Indian who had come from Black Birch Lake to meet us, laughed a little but had nothing to offer. Gus McDonald, the province's wise and gentle Commissioner of Fisheries, had no solution. Jim Langford, the youthful deputy minister of public works, said he could get better fishing in Wascana Slough, within a stone's throw of the Parliament buildings in Regina. An energetic young architect, used to getting results, he was trying hard to keep an open mind about this distant journey in search of a small fish, but it was only respect for our advanced years that kept him from declaring the whole project a romantic aberration—which I suppose, and hope, it was.

Fishing on the far side of the pool next morning with Albert, Norm Ferrier solved the main problem rather quickly. He had some small rubber or plastic nymphs, unlikely looking creatures which flopped heavily into the water and sank quickly. Casting these upstream into the easy current of a lesser run between the little islands, Norman let them well down on the swing, then retrieved very slowly and smoothly. And the grayling took them, usually on the slow retrieve, especially a white one that could easily be seen through ten feet of water. He soon had a fine catch of fish running around two and a half to three pounds.

While Norman was doing this I waded well out into the white water at the foot of the rapids. I had risen at least one grayling to a floating fly on the first afternoon and wanted to see if they wouldn't be doing a little better today. They weren't. I rose and hooked one nice fish of two and a half pounds and managed to get one or two other half-hearted rises, but it was a slow business. Though it was June, the Careen Lake country was still in the earliest stages of spring. The birches had not yet put out leaves; insects—even mosquitoes—were few and far between; the main body of the lake, except for a few feet along the shoreline, was still solid ice; the grayling like the rest of the land about them, were stirring only slowly towards the activity of summertime.

I let my little dry fly pull under and drift down in the white water. It was taken almost at once by a strong fish that ran downstream a good fifty yards. There the fly came away. I brought it back and threw it into the white water again. The same thing happened, but this time I landed a handsome, broadsided whitefish of over three pounds.

From then on almost every cast that reached new water took a fish, usually a whitefish but occasionally a grayling. Any small fly, No. 12, 14 or 16, was taken, if not eagerly, at least in a businesslike way. And the whitefish were worthy performers. They were a very level lot, all about eighteen inches long, but varying in weight from two and three-quarters to three and a half pounds. They ran strongly in the heavy water, not fast but in short determined bursts that took out line with complete authority. They came back, or rather were worked back, in much the same way, now yielding a few feet, now turning down to take out line again; always they found time to slam their heavy tails against the leader and very often they rolled, suddenly and awkwardly; right to the very end they would not give in and the small hooks tore out of their soft mouths very easily, so it took some while to collect enough of them to satisfy Norman and Albert.

Later, while Norman and I made little holding pools and tried to get good color photographs of the fish, Ann tried Norman's method for the grayling, while Albert stood by with the net. She did well and finished with the largest grayling we caught, a fish of three and a quarter pounds.

In a sense, I suppose the Black Birch grayling should have been a disappointment to me. I had pictured a stream where I could work up from pool to pool, finding grayling in each coming readily to surface flies. I had dreamed of fish surpassingly beautiful, brighter than the Coppermine fish and with violet-blue lights all through them; much larger than the Parsnip River fish and with dorsal fins as nobly tall and turquoise-spotted as those of Coppermine—all the possible beauties combined and enriched, and perhaps the chance of a record fish as well. The Black Birch fish were quite dark, with only a suspicion of purple lights along their sides; their tails were rusty red and something of the same color was along the backs of many of them; their dorsal fins were enormous, handsomely spotted with turquoise, but rather often split or frayed.

Yet I was perfectly happy with them. We were a little too early in the season to see them at their best, that was all. The compensations were innumerable. It was good to know that grayling are not always wide open to a simple dry fly technique, good to see them in their spring lethargy and to see how little their recent spawning had reduced them. I was even glad to have seen a new color range, although an inferior one. And watching their slow, shadowy movements deep in the water under the slowly drawn white nymph was a delight.

Albert was one of the best and pleasantest guides I have ever known. He is a big, handsome, well-built man who fishes through each winter in the north country with his wife and children and returns to Ile-á-la-Crosse, a hundred miles due south of Black Birch, in the late spring. He talks very little, yet will always answer a question. He offers no advice and seems almost to disregard the whole process of fishing; yet every so often he points out a fish or the movement of a bird or a gull's nest on a rock, something one might have missed without him. He was always ready with the net when the time came, yet never too soon with it. His movements were calm, unhurried and sure. And for all his apparent unconcern he had always a smile of gentle satisfaction for a good fish.

Albert had quick eyes for fish and several times he showed me grayling deep in the water so that I could follow their movement through a longish reach where the light was good. Most of these seemed not to be feeding. They swam very slowly and near bottom, their dorsal fins swaying occasionally so that the turquoise of the spots shone up through ten feet of dark water. A few, I thought, must still be spawning, because I saw an occasional flash as they turned on their sides and, once or twice, saw males chasing each other.

We all caught grayling that second day and for Jim Langford it was not only his first grayling, but his first fish of any kind on the fly. Wascana Slough no longer looked like the dear lost waters of youth. Jim was a happy man. For that matter we were all happy and much too relaxed to go back over the short trail across the isthmus to the grayling pool after supper. Norman suggested that a few lake trout might be moving into the shallows where the ice had broken away from the edge of the lake. So Jim and Ann and I went in the canoe with Albert and cruised slowly along between the edge of the ice and the reedy shoreline. Jim was casting a spoon in the hope of pike or lake trout. I was casting a small streamer fly with the same hope in lesser degree.

It was a very beautiful, very still evening and the feel of

the northern country was in everything about us, exciting and deeply moving. Perched on the topmost tip of little spruce trees, the Canada birds sang their clear trilling flute-song over and over, ending always with the whistled "can-a-da-can-ada." Beyond us, along the north side of the lake, a carnival of loons, newly arrived from the south, was flying and splashing and crying in a hazy light that magnified the birds and dramatized all their vigorous movement. Gulls quarreled on the little islands, where some already were nesting, Arctic terns swept over us in graceful flight, frogs croaked harshly along the shoreline and a beaver slapped his tail and disappeared in a line of bubbles. An occasional pair of mallards rose sharply away from us, in shallow places jackfish swirled now and then and Jim cast his spoon at them.

I cast to the ice edge, let the fly sink down and draw round as Albert gently paddled the canoe through the still water. Every twenty or thirty feet I retrieved and cast again. Nothing was farther from my thoughts than fish. I had decided long ago that if the flash of Jim's spoon could move nothing, my little twist of tinsel and strand of mallard was swimming strictly for exercise. I suppose I was talking to Ann or looking over my shoulder at the loons when it happened. With a suddenness I expect only from summer steelhead, my little fly rod was jerked almost out of my hand, in the same moment the reel was running as though the ratchet would tear out of it. It ran and ran, along the edge of the ice at first, then under it, pulling down deep. The end was as sudden as the beginning. Everything stopped. I recovered line as fast as I could, but there was no resistance and soon the little fly came twinkling along close under the surface with nothing to suggest what had so fiercely attacked it.

I am used to fishing alone and saying what I like in moments of stress, so the violence of the unexpected action had stirred an equally violent reaction of unprintable words from me. Ann very properly reproved me. Jim looked a little startled, but realized the stress had been formidable. Only Albert was unmoved, or did he smile a little? Had it been a lake trout or a pike? A lake trout, I supposed, though there was no possible way of knowing. The quiet of the evening returned to us, with the sun lost under the red sky to the west. Jim and I cast with a new enthusiasm, but nothing ventured to disturb us again and we didn't care very much.

There are thousands of lakes like Careen and thousands of streams like the Black Birch across the northern reach of Canada's three prairie provinces. They are part of that immense complexity of waterways which the fur traders used on their journeys to and from Hudson's Bay and Montreal. Nearly all the lakes hold northern pike and whitefish and lake trout. Most of the streams must surely hold grayling and most are completely untried by anglers. There should be grayling of every shape and color and size among them, some perhaps more beautiful than any man's eyes have yet seen. Somewhere in the wilderness between Careen Lake and la Ronge we passed over two lakes that were brilliantly blue-green among the blues and browns of all the others. What, I wonder, would be the color and sheen of their grayling?

PART FIVE

Signs of the Times

1. *The Lawbreaker*

I DREAMED ONE NIGHT I WAS WATCHING A
pleasant stream—obviously, I decided, a good trout stream.
As I watched, a long-legged old character waded into the
stream and began fishing a dry fly over the tail of the pool.
He was a skillful and graceful fisherman, yet there was
something awkward about his movements. As his fly lighted
he hunched his shoulders almost as though he were trying
to hide what he was doing. A small fish rose, he carefully
avoided striking it as any good fisherman would—then
glanced quickly, and, I thought, apprehensively, behind
him. Still holding the fly in the air with false casts, he looked
searchingly up and down both banks before shooting it out
again.

As he worked on upstream and began to search the run under the far bank he seemed to relax a little and begin enjoying himself. He was doing a beautiful job, covering each and every likely holding place with perfect, drag-free drifts. He kept his small fly cocked and floating like a natural, lifting it without the least disturbance and setting it down again so lightly that it seemed to have floated into place. Several times he deliberately missed or shook off small fish, and each time he stopped for the same furtive glance at the woods along the banks.

Halfway up the run he rose a nice fish of fourteen or fifteen inches, which he knocked on the head and slipped into his creel. A few feet farther on a still better fish took the fly. The old man handled him like an artist, controlling his rushes, drawing him steadily downstream and away from the unfished water until he was ready for the net. It was as he slipped this fish into his creel that I saw the slow, quiet rise at the head of the pool.

The old man saw it too. His back stiffened, he stared closely at the spot where the fish had risen, then calmly set about changing his fly. I knew it was a good fish, because I had risen and pricked it in the same place about a week earlier; it was not only a good fish, it was probably the best in the river—five pounds anyway, perhaps nearer six.

The old fisherman didn't waste time on the rest of the pool. He moved up slowly and carefully into position, watching the water with such close concentration that the furtive awkwardness of his earlier movements completely disappeared. The big fish rose again. The old fisherman stripped two or three more yards of line from his reel, keeping the fly swinging back and forth in smooth easy false casts. The rod came forward in a low arc and a

moment later the fly was dancing easily down the gentle
riffle at the head of the pool. The rise came again, the fly
disappeared, the rod lifted slowly and easily to set the hook
in the big fish. Then the reel was screaming and the head
of the pool was foaming.

The old man's movements remained calm and unhurried,
but they were effective; very soon he had coaxed the fish
back into the body of the pool and was controlling his sharp
strong rushes towards the roots and snags of the far bank.
In a surprisingly short time the fish began to tire, rolling his
great side out of the water, slapping his broad tail as he
turned down for another short, angry run. Still the old man
did not hurry, but the runs grew shorter and shorter, the
swirls less and less violent and at last the fish was lying
quietly on his side in the shallows. Gently the old man drew
his head up on to the gravel bar, let him kick himself still
farther up, then bent down and freed the hook. He put his
rod down, slid the fish carefully back into the water and
stood there nursing it back to life, completely absorbed.

Only then did I notice a second figure on the gravel bar.
A big man, dressed in the forest-green of the Game Commission's uniform, was standing just behind the old fisherman, looking down at him. The game warden reached out
a hand and touched the fisherman's shoulder. The old man
gave the fish a firm push, then straightened up.

"Good afternoon," he said.

"Good afternoon, sir," said the game warden. "Been
watching you the last hour. I'm afraid I'll have to take you
in. You know better than turn back a fish like that."

"I'm sorry. I thought someone else might have a bit of
fun with him one day."

"Fun? On a trout stream? Don't you know a big fish like

that is just a nuisance? Chases the little fish, eats up all the grub, too cagey to take anything with a hook in it. And if some guy is unlucky enough to latch on to him all he'll get is his tackle busted and his efficiency reduced."

"Efficiency?" The old man looked puzzled.

"Sure. Harvesting efficiency. How do you think we're ever going to harvest the crop with guys like you putting fish back. And that isn't all. Look at your gear there. Fly. Floater at that. Same section of the act, but heavier penalty."

"I'm sorry, Warden. I didn't know about that."

"No? Seems to me I've warned you before. 4x gut. You know that's out. Illegal hook size, too—can't be more than No. 14. Section 23 says no hook smaller than No. 6. Then I'll have to book you for returning small fish too."

The old man brightened a little at that. He looked almost crafty. "But I didn't return any small fish."

The game warden laughed. "You can tell that to the judge. Maybe he'll believe you. Section 24 says three fish missed on the strike puts the onus on the accused to prove he wasn't returning them. I seen you miss six in a row. An old fellow like you ought to know better."

The old man looked completely defeated now. "I know it, Warden. But I won't be around so much longer. I thought I'd like to go out just once again and fish like a sportsman."

The game warden shook his head in wonder. "I just thought that might be it. Sport! Seems like you old-timers'll never learn. Must be five years since the last one of you was pinched. Commissioner thought he had it stamped out. Wait till he hears about this. It'll mean life, for sure."

"In jail?" asked the old man.

"I should say not. Working on the crop. From now on you'll be following every tank truck from the hatchery and using salmon eggs on every plant until you die. Might be commutation for efficiency, but you better be good. Competition's pretty hot. There's plenty of natural good citizens follow the trucks and those boys pick 'em up fast. Come along now. I'll take the gear. Important evidence."

I put it down as a dream at the time, or a nightmare maybe. Now I'm not so sure. It seems more like prophetic fantasy. A few months later I was reading the regular bulletin of the Washington State Fly-Fishing Club, and it became evident that my vision was more prophetic than fantastic.

"We well know that the practice of releasing trout is not approved of by the Department of Game. To return fish to the water is to oppose "The Harvest." Trout are to be caught and to be killed. Every one. Holdovers are an accident—an unfortunate accident. Ideally, every legal sized trout should be caught and killed each year. . . . Until lately this disapproval has been rather informal, and only half-serious. A few weeks ago, in one district, the District Supervisor stated he would arrest any angler caught releasing fish. This statement has not been contradicted. Question, and you will be told that it is illegal to release legal sized trout . . . of one thing we may be sure, this talk of the illegality of releasing trout is aimed at one method—fly-fishing."

Tempora mutantur, nos et mutamur in illis. Or do we, will we? Can the leopard change his spots or the old dog learn new tricks, especially when the biscuits are made of sawdust? It seems unlikely. Perhaps it will simply add a new dimension of youth to the sport of our old age. There was a time when outwitting the game warden, or thinking he was outwitted, was the prettiest pleasure of all. I think I know ways—of course I know ways it could be done. If, in the days to come, my ways along the stream become a little furtive, if I glance rather often in search of hidden watchers along the bank, I shall merely be recapturing the lawbreaking apprehensions of my youth, and having a wonderful time.

2. *Fish Derbies*

I DARESAY THERE IS NO REASON WHY A man shouldn't have an innocent little flutter on the outcome of a fishing expedition, if he is inclined that way. Similarly, there's nothing against a good big lottery that encourages a mass fishing expedition, especially on the salt water or an overstocked lake. Fishing is a chancy business at the best of times, far less predictable than an honest horse race or an honestly balanced roulette wheel, and good people everywhere love to take chances on something chancy, the chancier the better. They also like to get something for nothing and, almost equally well, to get nothing more than a bit of fun and excitement for something expended. All in all, though it can make trouble at times, this is one of the more attractive characteristics of human nature. All in all, I can admire it freely because I am too tight-fisted to risk a dollar raise on a full house in a simple draw poker game.

But out on the Pacific Coast we always have to do things up bigger and better than anyone else. After all, we have the biggest salmon runs, the most rain, the highest dams, the most divorces and the craziest politics, so why not everything else? This fine broad spirit has produced also the biggest salmon derbies with the fanciest prizes in the history of mankind. The promoters have given away just about everything on the continent except the Statue of Liberty in New

York harbor and the Peace Tower at Ottawa, but they still hope to do better and they usually do every year. Contestants are numbered not by hundreds, nor by thousands, but by tens of thousands, which isn't too surprising with a brand-new convertible or a small yacht ready to go as reward for catching a nice fat salmon during a pleasant day on the water.

Very naturally, all this has led to some sharpish practice from time to time. After one big derby the judges noticed that some of the winning fish were unnaturally stiff and dry. A few inquiries revealed that they had been bought a day or so earlier from Indian commercial fishermen, buried on nearby beaches and picked up during the course of "derby day" by their provident and ambitious purchasers. On the face of it, this process looked to be far more certain and far less trouble than just dragging a hook and line around and hoping. But it didn't win any prizes and ended with fraud charges and rather lengthy jail sentences. However, it opens a fascinating field of speculation. May not some other piscatorial pilferers at other times have been more successful in pulling the scales over the judge's eyes? If all we fishermen are liars, as the authorities insist, surely some of us can be counted on to bring tangible proof of it in good condition.

But all the problems of a great salmon derby are not so simple as fraud, though most have their root in what psychologists would call over-stimulated acquisitive tendencies. A few years ago a friend of mine, a pleasant, competent individual and something of a fisherman himself, agreed to act as a judge in one of the great derbies. He emerged from the experience a badly shaken and somewhat wiser man; in

addition he had a fish story or a fishing story, or at any rate
a story connected with fishing of a sort, to touch the least
sympathetic heart.

My friend, whom we will call Tom Jones, is a man of
dignity and moderate substance, courteous, well-spoken,
diplomatic—altogether the sort of man who can be counted
upon to judge any contest of normal proportions whether
among beauty queens, prize steers or marbles champions,
with distinction and credit both to the contest and himself.
A contest among such good, simple, unassuming souls as a
bunch of fishermen should have been, for Tom Jones, a
piece of cake, or, less elegantly, duck soup. Yet, as I have
already suggested, he will probably bear the mental scars
of this one to his dying day.

On the day of the great contest, Tom found himself
comfortably established aboard the judges' launch, a well-
appointed yacht with a good supply of refreshments, a
spacious and comfortable after-deck and a general air of
appropriate dignity. Tom was, I gather, the junior judge.
He makes very little mention of his brother judges except
to suggest that from time to time one or other of them
pushed him forward into the fray. After all, they were
experienced men.

The judges' launch was anchored in the midst of several
thousand contestants, all paddling around in small boats in
search of a prize-winning monster. The prizes were impressive, starting out with a brand-new, fully equipped
convertible automobile, ranging down through four or five
more automobiles, also brand-new and fully equipped, but
not convertible except for cash, through boats and outboard
motors and shotguns and fishing gear and portable stoves

to, I suspect, free dinners at Joe's Diner and tickets to the local burlesque show. Most of them, including the five or six automobiles, were displayed on the weighing-in deck.

It was a lovely day and there was really very little for the judges to do except admire their surroundings and partake of refreshment until the closing time of the contest. Now that closing time was set for a certain hour, known to all contestants, and at that hour the closing was to be signaled by the firing of a gun. And no fish boated thereafter would qualify for that gleaming array of prizes whose listing would have taxed the author of the Book of Revelation.

As the closing hour drew near, it became evident that one boat, with a man and a woman in it, was still fighting a big fish at some little distance from the judges' launch. Word from one of the stewards of the contest confirmed this and the judges went into consultation. It was agreed to hold the firing of the gun and give the woman a chance to boat her fish. The appointed moment passed. Then five minutes. Then ten minutes and the woman seemed no nearer the end of her struggle.

"Go on out there, Tom," said one of the senior judges. "Tell her she's overtime already but we'll give her five more minutes. If she isn't through then, the gun goes anyway."

Cheerfully, in his innocence perhaps even glad of something to do, certainly glowing with a cozy sense of the generosity of the message he was carrying, Tom jumped into the steward's boat and they made for the scene of the engagement. As they approached, the man at the oars frantically waved them away. The steward slowed his motor and kicked out the clutch.

"Get away from here, you crazy so-and-so's," yelled the man at the oars. "Can't you see my wife's got a big fish on?"

Tom stood up to do his part. "I'm afraid you're over-time," he yelled back, as gently as the distance would allow. "The judges say they'll give you five more minutes, then they have to fire the gun."

The woman said her say then. "Don't you try to hurry me, you big boob. I've had this fish over an hour and I'm going to land it if it's the last thing I do."

The steward's boat had crept a little closer by now.

"I'm sorry, ma'am," said Tom in his most diplomatic voice. "I don't want to hurry you, but if you don't boat the fish before the gun, it won't qualify."

"Leave her alone," said the man at the oars. "What're you trying to do? Scare her into losing it? Tell the judges to hold the gun."

All this while the line was stripping off the reel in fierce, heavy jerks, being reeled back, stripping off again. Tom, being himself a fisherman, noticed that the boat seemed to drift very little, in spite of the heavy tide that was running. He noticed, too, that the line stripped off when the man rested or pulled on his oars, came back on to the reel when-ever he backed up to keep pace with the run of the fish.

"Jack," he said to the steward. "Let's run over there and see if we can get a look at that fish."

Jack speeded his motor a little and they ran over in the direction of the straining line. Fortunately the increased sound of the motor drowned out much of the vituperation showered upon them by the embattled couple in the row-boat. Tom stood up and peered into the water as they ap-proached the spot where the fish should be. Suddenly he

saw a dark shadowy mass several feet down in the water.
"Hold it, Jack," he said. "See what I see?"

"Yes," said Jack. "Kelp. And there's the spoon."

And there it was, shining from the depths like gold,
securely hooked in the bulb at the head of the waving
ribbons of weed.

"I'm afraid you're hooked in the kelp, ma'am," Tom said.
"If your husband will keep backing up on the oars you'll
find your spoon."

For answer the man dug his oars fiercely into the water.
The reel screamed and so did the woman. "Don't try to
give me that stuff," said the man at the oars. "Think I don't
know a fish when I hook one? Ain't no kelp can take line
off like that." He dug the oars again. The reel screamed
again. "Wow!" said the man. "Look at the bastard go."

Tom shrugged his shoulders. "I'm sorry, sir. We'll have
to fire the gun."

That was when the line broke. "Now look what you
done with your pestering. Made her bust it. She'd a'
won. . . ."

"Let's get out of here," said Tom. They turned for the
launch, the gun went off and the contest was over. But not
the judging.

As Tom left the steward's boat and started up the yacht's
companionway a number of small boats were converging
on the judges' launch. Tom saw a friend in one and made
the mistake of calling out to ask his luck. The friend held
up a little silvery grilse of about a pound.

"Here," he said. "Catch." And threw the grilse towards
poor Tom, who held out a hopeful hand, saw the little fish
arc over six feet short of it, splash into the water and sink.

The friend shrugged. "Out since before daylight and that's all I got to show for it."

"Too bad, Jim," Tom said. "You should've hung on to him. He'd have made a breakfast anyway. See you on the wharf."

Back at the wharf things were busy. There was a big fish on the scales, stiff as a board, the skin dry and wrinkled. It had been questioned. The judges crowded around it, felt it, consulted briefly, disqualified it. The man who had brought it in angrily muttered something about a lawsuit. The crowd milled around, a few laughed, one or two sympathized with the man. Everyone began to move over towards the five or six shiny new cars and a small raised platform near them.

"You'll be giving out the main prizes, Tom," said the senior judge. "Just the automobiles. They collect the others on vouchers from the weighing station. Better get started right away. The dealers are up there with the keys. Here's the list."

"Okay," Tom said and started obediently towards the stand.

"Give out the first prize for ladies first," said the senior judge. "Makes a nice little touch of courtesy. Then the convertible for the open prize."

"Good idea," said Tom. "I'll do that." He began to push his way through the crowd. Almost at once he came face to face with his friend, Jim, who had thrown the grilse towards him.

"What did you drop that fish for, you big lug?" said Jim. "It was good for an over-and-under shotgun."

"Gee, that's tough. I'm sorry. But it didn't come any-where near me."

"You let it slip right through your hands, that's all." Tom glanced at his friend, saw he wasn't kidding and pushed on. Somewhere behind him he heard a familiar voice.

"That's the guy made my wife lose her big fish. That's him."

Tom tried not to hear, made his way to the platform and shook hands with the automobile dealers. Then he made a short speech and announced the winner of the lady's first prize—Mrs. Kiddlestone, with a king salmon of twenty-six pounds eleven ounces. Mrs. Kiddlestone, a large, petulant-looking woman in her mid-thirties, untidily dressed in a sweater and slacks and high heels, came forward to the stage. Tom shook her hand and congratulated her amid cheers and applause, then asked her to pick out one of the five sedans. Without the slightest hesitation Mrs. Kiddle-stone turned and pointed a large finger at the convertible.

"I'll take that one, thank you," she said.

"I'm sorry, ma'am," Tom said. "But that is the open first prize. You have the choice of these over here."

"I get to choose first, don't I?" asked Mrs. Kiddlestone. "I'll take that one. Gimme the keys." Again, she indicated, very positively, the convertible.

The crowd began to murmur. "What's the hold-up?" "Give her the keys." And the unmistakable voice came from somewhere in the background. "See? What'd I tell you? That's him. That's the guy made my wife lose the big fish."

Mr. Kiddlestone came to the platform. He was smaller

than Mrs. Kiddlestone, sandy-haired and freckled. He pointed to the ranked and gleaming sedans. "It's one of those, dear. The convertible is for the open."

"Now, Harry, you keep out of this," said Mrs. K. "The man give me first choice and I took it. That's the one I want and they ain't going to put me off with any other."

"I'm sorry, ma'am," Tom said again. "Here are the keys to your car. I'm afraid I must get on with the prize-giving."

Mrs. Kiddlestone turned haughtily away. "May as well choose, honey," Mr. Kiddlestone told her. "You'll be left till last if you don't."

"I've made my choice, Harry, and they ain't going to put me out of it." She stamped her foot and folded her arms across her formidable chest.

Tom took the opportunity to whisper to one of the dealers: "Get the open-prize guy up here, quick."

It was done while Mrs. K.'s back was still turned. Tom wasted no time on formalities. He congratulated the man briefly, then added: "Here are the keys. Get down there quick, jump in and drive off."

The man glanced apprehensively at Mrs. K.'s angry back, nodded and was on his way. Tom began to announce another prize winner. With a sense of relief he heard the convertible's motor start. A moment later there was a piercing scream from Mrs. K. and her high heels were clattering down the steps from the platform. She landed on the dead run. But the first-prize winner was wasting no time either. The convertible took off, swung for the gateway and the open street. Mrs. K. gave it the back and the front of her tongue, but long before she could reach the gate it was out of sight and headed for its new home.

Tom got the rest of the prizes away without further incident but an hour later he was still at the wharf entrance. It was dark and the street lights were on. The last sedan still stood just inside the gate. Tom's brother judges had remained unheard from and invisible since the start of the prize giving. The crowd had long since left. Mrs. Kiddlestone was sitting on the curb, her head bowed on her arms, her powerful shoulders heaving with sobs of grief and fury. Mr. Kiddlestone stood hopelessly beside her. Tom was weary but still conscientious.

"Mr. Kiddlestone," he suggested. "Perhaps if you took the keys and started the motor Mrs. Kiddlestone would feel better."

Mrs. K.'s head jerked up. She tossed the hair back from her eyes. "You do that, Harry, you just do that and I won't never speak to you again."

Tom thought of suggesting to Harry that the bargain might not be a bad one, but he couldn't see adding to Harry's troubles. He bent down and placed the car keys gently on the curb beside Mrs. K. "I'll just leave them there," he said. "I'm afraid I'll have to be going now." And he went.

It is a fishing story, I suppose, but it hasn't much to do with the gentle pastime that Walton knew, nor with the gentle and humane spirit that the pastime is supposed to induce. I asked Tom what became of the car. He said he didn't know, never asked and never went back. He supposed they took it in the end.

The trouble is that big prizes bring out people who want nothing but big prizes. Even so, a big fancy derby can be a lot of fun and a fine spectacle for anyone who likes to be out on the water and doesn't care about prizes, large or small. For all I know it may be a lot of fun for people like Mrs. K. who do most earnestly want the big prizes. After all, there's nothing like a bit of yelling as a good way to limber up the emotions, especially if there's a brand-new sedan waiting outside the front door next morning. But on the whole I think little derbies and little prizes are more fun, and it's no bad idea to stay away from judging even those if you can.

3. *Less Time Between Bites*

THE BIG NEW FORCE IN FISH AND WILD-
life management is unquestionably the conception that any
given area of land or water will support only a limited
population of the desired creatures. It may be a large population or a small one, depending on feed, climate and other
conditions, but if it passes a certain limit either a natural
die-off or a deterioration of stock, or both, will occur.

This is most readily shown in the case of deer populations
in areas of heavy snowfalls. Given ample summer range
and good conditions, deer will become very abundant,
especially if new ranges have recently been opened to them
by logging and fire, and there has been a succession of easy
winters. As soon as this happens, the range is overpopulated,
because the true control is not the summer range at all, but
the normal winter range. Immediately the herds become
concentrated on this by normal or severe winter conditions, three control factors begin to work: there will be a
heavy die-off, the average size will decrease and reproduc-
tion will fall off. This last is the most serious factor because
it means that does will not be producing fawns until they
are two or three years old instead of at the end of their
first year; and even then they are likely to produce only
one instead of two fawns, and there may be heavy mor-
tality among these single fawns.

In other words, a heavy winter carryover after the hunting season puts an excessive strain on the winter range and results in a poor crop of fawns the following spring. A smaller carryover will produce just as many fawns, probably more, and the whole herd will be healthier and stronger. More important still, there will be far less risk of progressively overbrowsing the winter range from season to season and so compounding the problem.

Sound management of a deer herd therefore calls for cropping back to the right proportion for its winter range before winter sets in. There is nothing new about this. In one form or another, it has been a practice in European deer forests for many years. In North America it is comparatively new and based on thorough scientific investigation. Generally the biologists have tried to achieve heavier cropping by extending seasons and removing restrictions, especially the "bucks only" law, and the results have been highly successful.

Game fish management faces somewhat the same problems. We have long known that a heavily overstocked lake produces nothing but small fish, and those probably in poor condition. A given area of water can only produce so many pounds of fish per season, whether they are distributed among an abundance of small fish or smaller numbers of comparatively large fish. In an artificially stocked lake one simply increases or decreases the annual stocking to bring about a change in the desired direction. In a wild lake, blocking off spawning areas will reduce numbers and increase size, while improving spawning areas or supplementary stocking will produce more fish of smaller size. Adequate cropping by anglers is also important to ensure that a good proportion of the older fish are caught up and faster-growing young fish have a chance to come on.

Streams are a much more complicated and difficult matter. Here again it is possible to arrive at a figure for what should be the annual yield in pounds per acre. It is possible to increase the yield by stocking with fish of takeable size, and still more by improving the physical conditions of the stream itself. But streams have a limiting factor that is very much like the winter range of the deer—their periods of low flow. Low flow periods occur in winter freeze-up and in summer drought and their effect is obvious—the area and volume of water available to fish and insect life is drastically reduced, for a shorter or longer period. Prolonged summer drought, when the fish are normally more active than in winter, temperatures are higher and oxygen content lower, may cause serious losses simply through starvation. Winter dry periods may expose spawning beds and kill off the incubating eggs or alevins. In streams dependent on migratory stocks of salmon or trout the periods of low summer flow are probably the most important single factor in determining the size of future runs. The stream's capacity to raise fry and fingerlings to migrant stage is reduced almost exactly in proportion to the length and severity of the summer drought.

This is a highly simplified account of some of the issues that have to be faced in the management of a game fishery; and it is enough to explain why fisheries biologists are following the philosophy of game biologists and urging anglers to "take the crop" by lengthening seasons and removing restrictions such as size limits and catch limits. In overstocked lakes, which produce a low quality of fishing in any case—and a great many lakes are overstocked—this makes some sense, though control of spawning or some attempt to improve the lake's capacity would make more. In lakes subject to serious winter kill, as is sometimes the case where heavy snowfalls cover the ice and cut out all light, the policy makes sense. In "put and take" lakes entirely maintained by annual plantings, where a high yield of numbers to an intensive fishery is the sole object, it is obviously desirable. On lakes that are already in good balance, yielding satisfactory proportions of the various age classes, it serves no useful purpose at all and may do serious damage.

In streams, some of the same arguments apply as in lakes. A "put and take" stream, for what it is worth, will produce most efficiently if its entire stock can be caught up each year. A stream where there is serious winter kill can only produce usefully if it is regularly stocked, and I suppose it is logical to feel that hatchery fish left to die a natural death without reproducing themselves are wasted. But a stream that provides a good, well-balanced natural fishery can be far more quickly ruined by excessive cropping than a well-balanced lake.

In migratory streams the argument is a little different. In the case of a good steelhead stream, for instance, it will be argued that more fish than are necessary for the future, escape to the spawning beds and spawn successfully. Their too abundant progeny, which must grow through two years of fresh-water life, crowd each other out and many die of starvation during the low flow periods of the stream. These, like the excess spawners which produced them, represent "waste." Therefore restrictions should be removed and anglers should be encouraged to take the crop by every possible means short of gill-nets and dynamite. They may even be encouraged to take the young six- or eight-inch steelheads on their downstream migration and call it "trout fishing."

Most of the arguments about harvesting the run or taking the crop make a measure of sense—some more, some less—if one accepts a single premise: that the main purpose of sport is killing. The logical mind of the scientist charged with the management of a fishery leads him into exactly this misconception.

"So," he says, "these people want to go fishing. Now why would anyone want to go fishing? To catch fish, of course." And he begins to measure the angler's success or failure—and his own success or failure—in terms of fish per fisherman hour. The excellent bulletin of the Sport Fishing Institute, which is a sort of round-up of game fish management activities throughout the United States and Canada, carries a motto just below its masthead: "To Shorten the Time between Bites."

The only trouble with this conception is that it has absolutely nothing to do with the sport of fishing. Few things concern an enthusiastic fisherman less than the length of time between "bites." If asked he would probably say: "Lengthen the time if you like. But give us bigger fish and more difficult fish, under more romantic and exciting circumstances."

The biologist believes he can have no time for this sort of thing. He is burdened with the awful pressure of numbers: hundreds of thousands, millions of Americans who want to go fishing and who must all catch fish unless he is to fail in his job. The answer of course is efficiency and a quick turnover; lots and lots of fish in readily accessible places, to be attacked promptly, if possible all the time and with the most efficient machinery that can still give some illusion of sport. The drill is pretty much that of the public pool in a trout farm: You've paid your money (bought your license, that is); now get in there fast, catch your fish and give someone else a chance.

The real truth is that sport is made by and exists in just three things: tradition, ethics and restraint. Reduce, remove or destroy these and nothing useful is left. It may be enough to satisfy newcomers to the sport for a little while, but it cannot hold them long—there will be nothing to grow on, nothing to advance to. In the end, if any real efficiency could be attained, the sport itself would die and be forgotten.

Even the deer hunter, who has a thousand times more reason to string along with the philosophy of "taking the crop" than the fisherman can ever have, cannot find what he wants in it. One old hunter put it to me squarely the other day: "Maybe a man oughter shoot does and fawns," he said. "I've got nothing against it. But when you see them horns, boy, that's what you come out for." My friend has killed his share of does in his time—there was the matter of eating during the depression—but they are not what he is looking for, and never will be.

To most fishermen beyond the elementary stage of things, there is neither sport nor satisfaction in six- or eight-inch fish. There is really nothing these tiny creatures can do to give sport or satisfaction. There is not much sport in catching fish, even fairly large fish, on gang trolls.

There is neither sport nor challenge, nor the sense of generosity to the quarry that goes with sport, in wide-open seasons, wide-open bag limits, wide-open size limits or wide-open tackle regulations. The sportsman soon realizes he is simply being maneuvered into increasing the biologist's apparent efficiency.

No one owes more to fish and game biologists than I do, no one has more respect for their skills. And I think I have done my little share towards bringing them to some of the honored positions they hold today. Scientific thinking has done wonders for them in their researches and explorations. They have already learned more than I expected would be known in my lifetime. But when they come to dealing with the intangibles of sport, which are a sizable section of human psychology, scientific thinking utterly betrays them.

What has to be understood is that the *quality* of sport is all-important. And the quality of sport is not something that can be readily measured; it is the sum of generations of tradition, ethics and restraint. The quality of sport is in what anglers themselves have imagined, developed, tested and proved over hundreds of years. It is something that has evolved, not something that has been imposed. It is in what a man dreams of by the fireside at home and goes out next day or next year to try and realize on his favorite lake or stream. Even the unsophisticated fisherman dreams, and his dreams are not of being bullied into taking the crop.

Biologists have, and always will have, a tremendous job to do in the management of public game fisheries; and they can do it far better than untrained minds, provided they first understand the real meaning and purpose of sport. It is not their business to change the desires of the angler to suit their own purposes; it is their business to recognize and understand these desires and then to provide for them so far as can humanly be done.

It is difficult to describe what I mean by "quality fishing" in broad general terms to fit all types of fishing and all types of water. It is fishing that sets problems and allows for, even demands, skillful performance; it implies preservation, so far as possible, of natural conditions in the waters, their surroundings and the fish themselves; it is fishing that falls within the limits of certain traditions, yet allows for growth and development; it is fishing where unexpected things can and do happen, fishing where a man has room to move and think and see and hear and be himself.

This is a big order and it is perhaps impossible to achieve in most waters that are readily accessible to large urban populations; but even here something can be done by recognizing the claims of minorities who want some sort of quality. Away from the big cities, North America is still a very large continent. There is plenty of room for both quality fishing and elementary fishing. Many waters still provide quality fishing without the slightest aid or interference from man; it is important to preserve these. Many waters would still provide quality fishing but for the interference or mismanagement of man; it is important to restore these. Many waters could be made to provide quality fishing by proper regulation; it is important to regulate them.

Most game fisheries still need a great deal of fundamental

research work to determine fully the life histories and habits of their fish and the conditions that affect them. This is the first and most important place to spend money. Nearly all streams and many lakes can be physically improved to provide more and better fishing. This is the second place to spend money. Artificial hatching and rearing and planting on a put and take basis should always be a last resort; it should be limited to waters fit for nothing else or where fishing pressure makes anything else impossible.

Let the biologists read and learn their Juliana and Walton and Halford, their Gordon and Hewitt and LaBranche. They would know then that the holdover fish is not the villain of the piece, but the stuff of the angler's dreams. They would know there is more to fishing than fish and more to sport than filling a bag. They would know that sport without limits and restraints, without ethics and tradition, is not sport at all and can satisfy no thinking person for very long. And they would be well on the way to perpetuating the sport of angling and their own usefulness with it.

4. *The Great Destroyers*

I<small>N HIS HEEDLESS DAYS, WHICH ARE NOT</small>
yet over, man did a lot of damage to the face of the earth
by fire, by unwise clearing, by overgrazing, by polluting
and obstructing streams and by wanton destruction of both
fish and wildlife. We are wiser now. We recognize these
things as evils and pay at least some lip service to the idea
of avoiding or preventing them. In fact we have quite a
lot of legislation against such abuses and some of it actually
works.

But at the same time we have become killers and de-
stroyers on a much vaster and far more efficient scale. We
have entered upon a new stage of damaging the face of
the earth and too many of us regard it as a virtuous and
progressive phase, even as our fathers regarded those earlier
injuries and destructions.

I am not thinking at the moment of nuclear destruction,
poisoning or pollution, though that, as everyone knows,
offers the most efficient and progressive means of wiping
out everything—if it has not, in fact, begun the process
already. Simple fishermen have to face this issue in common
with the rest of mankind and bear their share in dealing
with it—though we might well remember as we do so, not
without bitterness, our brothers of the *Lucky Dragon*.
I am thinking now of simpler issues, ones we should face
and recognize and control without too much difficulty.

And the first and most deadly of these is the wholesale spraying of large areas of the countryside with poison.

DDT, like fire, is a friend of men if wisely used and rigidly controlled. DDT, like the original atom bomb, has still more fearful and deadly brothers and sisters, calling for yet wiser use and still more rigid control. One is called heptachlor and there are others, but the names don't matter much. What matters is that they are poisons which are sprayed from airplanes over great wide areas of land and forest and watershed to kill some specific pest like the fire ant or the hemlock looper or the spruce budworm; and in the process they are quite likely to kill or damage almost everything that walks or crawls or swims or flies. And the people who are killing their special pests couldn't care less, unless someone draws it forcefully to their attention. Even then they are likely to do no more than murmur a few polite condolences and get set to lay waste another few hundred thousands or millions of acres.

I have never yet met a forester who professed to know precisely what he was doing when broadcasting his pet poison over a great area of forest. Generally he expected to "control" the specific pest that was bothering him; how thoroughly or for how long, he did not know; what else might be killed, he did not know; what would be the effect of wiping out natural controls, such as birds and other insects, he did not know; how often the treatment would have to be repeated to compensate for such destruction, he did not know; how long its evil effects might persist, he did not know. Yet someone had given him permission to go ahead and do the damage.

And damage it most certainly is, probably to his own

interests as well as those of everyone else. The forest insects of course are killed, a number of them certainly predators, competitors or parasites of the very insect whose destruction is the purpose of the spraying. DDT in moderate concentration (one pound to the acre or less) probably does not destroy many birds or mammals. Heptachlor immediately destroys some 75 to 85 per cent of birds and small mammals and how much later damage it does, no one knows. But in the streams, where most of the stuff ends up after a bit of rain, the effects of them all are disastrous.

From DDT spraying near the Miramichi River in 1954, at a rate of only a half-pound to the acre, fingerling salmon were practically or completely wiped out. Of salmon parr only one in ten survived after three weeks. Nearly all aquatic insects completely disappeared. Three months after spraying, dead and dying salmon parr were still being found.

In spite of these grim results, it was decided to spray a forest area on the north end of Vancouver Island in the summer of 1957 with a dose of one pound of DDT to the acre. There are a number of highly productive trout and salmon streams in the area, including the Nimpkish, the Cluxewe and the Keogh. Of course, things would be different this time; certain precautions would be taken, streams would be avoided so far as possible, fisheries observers would supervise, all would be well. But it wasn't. Stream losses of young coho salmon, steelhead and cutthroat trout were as high as 95 per cent. Aquatic insects were destroyed and the productivity of the streams was set back, perhaps for years. Most local people believe the timber would have recovered from the budworm infestations, as it has before, and that any that did not recover could have been salvaged without serious loss. But then most of the local people are commercial fishermen.

So far forest-spraying of this type has not been too widely used. But enough has been seen of it to convince any thinking person that, apart from its other evils, it is terribly destructive to aquatic life. Repeated sprayings, which are all too likely to become necessary from the very nature of their effect, must inevitably destroy all stream and most lake life, including the anadromous species of commercial and game fish. It is an outrageously evil practice and no state or province should tolerate it. I sometimes think the remedy may lie in civil law, in suit by sportsmen or resort owners or commercial fishing interests for damage done. No doubt there are problems in this, but it is an elementary principle of justice that men must have right of legal redress when their interests are damaged by the actions of others. And I can think of nothing that would discourage the practice more quickly than the threat of a multiplicity of civil damage suits.

Another fine big means of destruction that has come into its own in the hands of modern man is the hydroelectric dam. Actually hydroelectric dams are a clumsy and outdated way of manufacturing power and many will be knocked down before long and the lakes behind them drained to recover the drowned land. But we haven't got to that stage yet; we are still busy building them and committing ourselves to primitive ways.

Not all hydroelectric dams are harmful and destructive to fish and wildlife; some are highly beneficial and create other important recreational assets as well. It is a complicated story, and sportsmen have to realize that each and every dam is a special problem of its own. One can of course lay down certain obvious principles: dams that block anadromous streams without providing safe passage up and down stream for migrants are evil; dams that damage the values of parks or wilderness areas are an outrage; dams that flood valuable agricultural land are fundamentally unsound; and no dam should be permitted to flood forest land unless a complete clearing job has been done in advance.

Sometimes a dam may improve conditions by providing a more even flow of water to the river below it, though flood control dams are far more reliable for this purpose than hydroelectric dams; sometimes a dam may greatly increase the yield of a lake by extending the area of shallow water and increasing the shoreline development; a dam on a lake that flushes out in, say, two or three weeks at the normal flow of the river will hold back the water and allow a great increase of plankton. But even advantages of this sort may be quickly counterbalanced by the destruction of aquatic life and the restriction of range during periods of draw down. These are the sort of things anglers should ask questions about, if they can get or make a chance to do so when dams are contemplated.

Low level dams on salmon streams can often be successfully by-passed by fishways and elevators, though there is always the difficult problem of steering downstream migrants past the turbine inlets. Unfortunately engineers are rarely content with one dam on a major river and they will always build a high dam if they can find a place for it. High dams and salmon, or a multiplicity of dams and salmon, simply do not go together. Much has been written of the Columbia, millions of dollars have been spent to compensate for its dams. But the fact remains that the greatest king salmon river in the world retains only the shadow of its greatness. Fish that once traveled twelve hundred miles to the foot of the Rockies can now only struggle through a fraction of that distance. Productive lakes and ideal spawning waters are forever barred to them. Twenty years ago the Columbia fish made up 65 per cent of the catch along the west coast of Vancouver Island and over 50 per cent as far north as Dixon Entrance. Today these figures are about 45 and 30 per cent respectively and still decreasing. And the engineers haven't yet finished with the Columbia system.

The greatest sockeye stream, and the greatest all-around salmon river still left is the Fraser in British Columbia. And the engineers have a mean and hungry eye upon it. They would like to build a 750-foot dam at Moran, just above the entrance of the Thompson, and a whole sequence of dams from there down. And, they say, the salmon men ought to be able to solve their problems and get their stupid fish up and down.

It is interesting to look at just a few of those problems. In the first place the water below the dam is likely to be as much as fourteen degrees colder than the water above it. That order of temperature change is, by itself, enough to kill fish outright. The water will also be fourteen degrees colder than the normal output of the Fraser at migration time and that may be quite enough to delay, if not to prevent, the fish coming up to the dam. As they come up they must be steered or blocked away from moving up into the tail race from the powerhouses, probably by another low dam. They must then be carried by fishways, elevators and locks through the 750-foot vertical lift over the face of the dam. At the peak of the run, these facilities would have to handle not less than three-quarters of a million fish a day. Any delay in handling would probably be fatal, as the upstream races of Fraser River sockeyes have a leeway of only some three to twelve days in the time they must reach their spawning grounds; some delay would be inevitable in collecting the fish, again as they sorted themselves out above the dam and still again in the passage through a 160-mile lake in the place of the old river bed, under different temperatures and oxygen conditions than they had ever known before. In addition, since the lake would be subject to a two-hundred-foot vertical fluctuation, all the fishways, elevators, locks and passes would have to operate at full efficiency anywhere throughout this range.

Assuming that all these problems are solved and the run gets up in some sort of fashion, which is quite unlikely, there is still a fascinating group of problems to be solved in getting the young fish down. In the first place there is no certainty that when they hit the big lake above the dam they will not decide to relax and stay there; it is more than likely that at least some of them would. If they let themselves be carried down by the current of the lake, its passage would take from two to four weeks, instead of the one or two days it now takes to pass through the same length of river. At the dam face they would have to be steered away from the spillways and turbine intakes, and no way has yet been found of doing this. They would also have to be guided into a by-pass of some kind, whose entrance would again have to operate over the two-hundred-foot range of possible fluctuation. The by-pass would have to carry them gently through the seven-hundred-and-fifty-foot vertical drop. And having done so it would immediately cast them out into water suddenly ten or fifteen degrees colder, which would probably kill them all. A very expensive death it would be, too, when one reckons up the cost of all the devices for getting their parents up and themselves down again, to say nothing of the cost of all the fish-boats that might as well be scrapped, the canneries that might as well be demolished, the people who would be that much hungrier and the sports fishermen who would probably take their troubles to the bars and liquor shops.

Fortunately British Columbia has several other major sources of hydroelectric power, including the Peace and the Upper Columbia, which will more than take care of her needs for the next twenty years. By that time nuclear power should be more than competitive with hydropower and far more economical and sensible in terms of distribution and land use than hydropower ever was. But that won't stop engineers and promoters and industrialists from trying hard to get hold of the Fraser. Somebody could make a lot of money out of a deal like that and what, after all, are a few fish, even the greatest salmon river in the world, alongside a promoter's dream?

The Adams River run brought back 18½ million fish to the Fraser this year. Less than a quarter of a million spawners in the Quesnel River, a tributary a little farther upstream, may bring back ten million in 1961. A big Chilco run is due in 1960. Thanks to the efforts of the International Pacific Salmon Commission, the Fraser is within sight of producing as it never has, even in the days before the white man came. As more and more is learned about improving spawning areas, about establishing and building new runs, about the rearing capacities and qualities of the lakes, the improvement should go on and on until the river system is not only the greatest salmon producer, but a far greater salmon producer than the world has ever seen before. And this is probably the best answer to the promoters and industrialists and engineers.

A solution to the problems of high dams on salmon streams is nowhere in sight. It may not be impossible—few things are. But it will never be found by mechanical means, by gadgets and guesswork and grandiose schemes to fool the public and quieten the consciences of the money-makers. It will be found, if anywhere at all, in the fish themselves. It is a matter for pure research, directed to learning exactly how and why the fish behave as they do. The interior and exterior forces of their migrations must be learned, the exact sources of their energy, the precise changes of body chemistry that carry them upstream to their spawning and certain death at a predetermined time. Somewhere in these things there may or may not be the answers to problems of high dams. It can be nowhere else.

5. *Access*

I AM OFTEN ASKED IF I DO NOT THINK
that the only future for hunting and fishing on the North
American continent is in private preserves. Even if I did
think so, there would be no point in thinking it. In the first
place, it is never likely to happen. In the second place, if
it did happen, only a tiny fraction of the people would be
able to hunt and fish and I not among them. And in the
third place a great ideal would have been lost.

As it is, we are in danger of losing the ideal already.
Every day more and more land and water is closed to the
public for one reason or another. Every day, so fishermen
tell me, they must go farther to find less. Every day the
streams and lakes and hunting grounds are more crowded;
or are they? I am not quite sure. Every day a few more
so-called sportsmen behave badly enough to put the whole
idea and ideal in jeopardy and to make it more nearly impossible for themselves, or anyone else.

But whose land is it? Whose game is it? Whose fish are
they? Everybody's. Let it stay that way. Let the timber-
man take his crop and only his crop. The land yields other
crops that he didn't buy with the timber, crops of fish
and wildlife. Let the farmer take his crop and the cattle-
man his, let the miner dig his minerals from under the
ground. Then let the hunter and the fishermen take their
crops, ethically, in sportsmanlike fashion and with a decent

regard for the other users of land and water. It is not impossible.

Access is the great new watchword of the North American sportsman. It means access to all lands and waters that are used for other purposes. Without it we shall be crowded, within a generation, into a few remaining parks and wilderness areas, and we shall in effect be crowded out of them.

Access is a freedom and, like other freedoms, it calls for constant vigilance. The best way I know to be vigilant and to support vigilance is to belong to a sportsman's organization. These can be tiresome or pleasant and entertaining. They can be strong or weak, informed or ignorant, rich or poor. But they all need members and they are the only power that can speak persistently and effectively for access.

Access in my country means mainly the right to travel over private logging roads. We fight and argue and negotiate for it, and generally we get it, in some form or another. We also fight for government to provide access, by building roads and trails and boat landings, by setting land and water aside, by buying access when it has to. It all goes very slowly, but it is a lot better than if we did nothing at all.

If we lose this broad principle of the right of all men to hunt and fish where they can do so without harm to others, it will be only a matter of time before the whole thing is gone. This is obvious enough—without land to hunt over and water to fish over there can be no hunting or fishing. The argument against access is usually the public abuse of the right—damage to crops, to machinery, equipment and buildings, damage by fire and litter. These are all good points. But the reverse of the picture was brought home to me by two instances last summer. In the first a great lake park had been closed to the public by a power development. Fire started in the timber and burned six thousand acres along the lake shore before it was brought under control. With the public in there the fire would have been promptly detected, promptly fought and promptly controlled; I know this, because other dangerous fires have started in other years and have been promptly controlled. The timber that was burned had stood for five or six hundred years—until they let industry in and kept the public out.

The other instance is a beautiful little summer steelhead stream, newly discovered. There are few like it and I have never seen a better one. The fish are abundant, they lie well in many places and come up to the dry fly as though trained to it. But the stream is tiny at summer level—a succession of deep pools and canyon water linked by boulder-strewn shallows one can cross dry shod. The way into it was by twenty-five or thirty miles of logging road. It was not hard to get permission to go in. Then, quite suddenly, policy changed and there was no more permission. I am not too concerned about this, because I think policy will change again, and in time. But I can remember other streams like this where runs were ruined before the public even saw them by dynamiting and other abuses that would be impossible except behind the shield of industrial privacy. I hope it will not happen here, but I shall be glad when the stream is open again—and not merely because I want to catch some more of its fish. I'd like to keep a friendly eye on it.

A lesser problem, but still an important one, is the proper distribution of sportsmen over areas of hunting or fishing country. Nothing destroys sport more surely than excessive crowding, and except in large areas, this should not be necessary. The ideal is to keep sportsmen spread and keep them moving. Streams are my own chief concern and I am now convinced that fly only should be the rule on all trout and steelhead streams at least during the summer months. This is not likely to come about very soon, but in the meanwhile a good proportion of streams should be set aside for fly only and the rest should be limited to fly or artificial lures. Bait is completely unnecessary and undesirable at any time of year for trout or steelhead, if only because bait fishermen can and do park in good spots and hold them all day. Fly- or spinner-fishermen, if they know their business at all, keep moving and give everyone a chance. They can also release small or unwanted fish with a 90 per cent better record of survival.

Wise planning of public campsites is still another means of distributing anglers, especially in lake countries. Far too often a popular lake, already being fished to something near its capacity, is overcrowded because the government decides to provide camp grounds for everyone. Usually, in British Columbia at all events, there are half-a-dozen lakes nearby, some of them probably quite as good, which are being underfished. Intelligent planning will always reach out to these, even if it costs a little more, rather than damage what is already good.

Outboard motors can be a great help at times. But on small trout lakes they are an abomination. Their noise and smell destroys all illusion of solitude. The surface film of oil a good number of them can produce on a small lake may be quite damaging to aquatic insects and even to vegetation. On lakes of one square mile or less they are not only totally unnecessary, but more destructive than beneficial even to those who use them. On lakes of four square miles or less motors should be limited to five horsepower or less; and even on large lakes the heavily fished shallows should be marked and all high-speed power boats should be made to keep outside the markers. There is plenty of water for both outboard enthusiasts and fishermen, and they don't need to be crowded into the same place. Generally the fisherman's interests are in the smaller lakes and limited areas of the larger ones. These should be protected for him.

I often wonder if we haven't just about reached the probable limit of angling pressure. The figures are formidable—well over thirty million angling licenses in the United States and Canada; with one possible exception, bowling, it is unquestionably the most popular sport in North America. And not so long ago the fisherman shuffled along, hiding his face and his gear in case someone should laugh at him.

Izaac Walton said, and I believe him: "Angling is somewhat like poetry, men are to be born so." I simply do not believe that thirty million North Americans and most of their children were born so; and I wonder how many of the millions have found any real pleasure and satisfaction in the sport?

In the years since the war, millions of people have found their way outdoors for the first time. They are still doing so, and probably in increasing numbers. Fishing is a natural and easy sport to turn to, at least at first, and it has become fashionable—a fad really. Certain improvements in tackle, such as the glass rod and the spinning reel with automatic pickup, have helped, and the popularity of boats and boating has also turned a certain number to the sport who might not otherwise have bothered with it. It would be nice if all these millions were to go on and develop into anglers in the true sense of the word, but it seems most unlikely that they will.

As time goes on I suspect that more and more of the glass rods and spinning reels will be left at home in the closet or carried unused in the back of the car or station wagon. Angling, after all, is a notoriously unrewarding sport in material ways and the angler is usually pictured as a disappointed man—which he often is, because no man can build his hopes higher or more foolishly, nor any man renew them so readily on such slight foundation. But it takes a little being "born so" to maintain this high faith in the totally improbable and I cannot believe that all the thirty million will continue to do so.

This may not mean any marked and sudden drop in the purchase of angling licenses, but I suspect that recruitment will slow up somewhat and the present great pressure on the game fish resources will gradually level off, if it is not already doing so. There are, after all, a tremendous number of other interests to compete as people get to know their way around the outdoors rather better—photography, botany, geology, bird-watching, boating, water-skiing, to name only a few—and many of these must have a good deal more to offer than the duller forms of angling.

If I am right about this, as I am pretty sure I am, I shall

be both glad and sorry. It has been an exciting thing to see the sport build up to its present popularity and it seems certain that an immense number of men and women have found true and lasting pleasure in it. But it seems just as certain that many others have lost their way in it. They have followed a fashion when one of the many other ways of enjoying the outdoors would have led them into far more intense pleasure and a much richer development. I wish them well and hope that, as they go about their new delights, they will remember with a touch of affection the sport that first took them outdoors.

PART SIX
Salt Water

1. *The Cruise*

I LIVE IN THE MIDDLE OF ONE OF THE
world's great salt-water fishing areas, probably the world's
greatest salt-water salmon-fishing area. When I first came
to it, I turned to it eagerly and found great sport in it.

But gradually I have turned away, back to the streams again or at best to the stream mouths and beaches.

I regret this, because there are many true delights in salt-water fishing—the moods of tide and weather, the colors of sea and sky, the seabirds and mammals, all the sights and smells and sounds of salt water. But a man has only a little time to spend on sport, and he had best spend it where he finds all his pleasures keenest. I hate trolling. And I find the confinement of a small boat very depressing after a while. If patience is a fisherman's virtue, I am not and never have been a virtuous fisherman. Even in a lake I prefer to hunt the stream mouths and wade the edges if it is at all possible.

A few years ago, Harold Stimson, Letcher Lambuth, Darrah Corbett and I went off for a few days on the salt water in Harold's most comfortable boat, the *Wanderer*. Since we were all confirmed fly-fishermen we had streams in mind for fishing rather than the salt water itself. Things didn't work out quite as we had hoped and we spent rather more time on salt water than we had expected.

It was late July and very hot weather. Our first idea was Theodosia Arm, which none of us had prospected before. It was an uncomfortable place to work into with a fifty-foot boat and the small-scale chart we had, but we got to the head without mishap and found a wide, grassy flat, with no significant stream running out across it. When we did find the Theodosia "river," it proved to be a small creek, so low at that season that its entire flow disappeared into a big gravel bar at the mouth. We decided it might offer something after the fall rains—a cutthroat run almost certainly and probably some cohos—but it was no place to waste time on just then.

Our next call was one that we had few doubts about—the Brem River, a fine little summer steelhead stream that flows into Salmon Bay on Toba Inlet. Darrah and I went ashore well-equipped and full of enthusiasm, while Letcher and Harold elected to work the bay for a chance at coho or king salmon. We had reckoned without the hot weather. The Brem is a glacial stream that runs clear much of the time; now it was running quite low, but carrying a heavy white silt that cut visibility to two feet or less. Still, it was a fine day to look over the stream, and we went off to do it.

The Brem drops through a tight narrow canyon about half a mile from the sea. Just below that is a big pool, broken up by huge boulders, where most of the fish are caught. More huge boulders block the canyon and the stream squeezes through them in little falls, so it seems likely that the fish only get through to the upper reaches in high water. An old logging road goes up along the left bank, so we decided to leave the big pool for later and look over the upper river.

Rather quickly we came upon signs of the valley's only inhabitant—a rusty cross-cut saw halfway through a cut in a small log at the side of the grade. An oil bottle hung beside it and the little pile of sawdust under the log was quite fresh; someone had started out the day with good intentions, found it rather warm and improved upon his intentions by wandering off.

"Quite a relaxed individual," Darrah suggested. "Whoever he is."

I agreed and pointed to the heavy-footed tracks leading

up the grade; the weight was on the heel and the outside of the foot, the steps short, with pebbles scuffed and turned between them. They suggested a big man ambling rather than walking. "Looks like we'll catch up to him pretty quickly," I said.

The valley was lovely in spite of the logging of a few years earlier. Alder and willow and small firs had grown back. The elderberries were ripening already and band-tailed pigeons clattered up from them in scores to the taller trees. The high mountains were close along either side and the mountain creeks had long ago torn away all the road bridges. Less than half a mile from his log we came upon the man of the saw. He was a huge, portly Indian, nearly six feet tall and something over two hundred and fifty pounds. His heavy woolen undershirt was open right to his waist and quiet rivers of sweat wandered gently over his smooth brown skin. He lowered himself to a seat on a convenient log as he greeted us.

"Any steelhead around?" we asked.

"A few maybe," he said. "Down by the canyon. Plenty humpbacks."

We were curious about a pool we had heard of called the Big Hole, though we suspected it might be someone's name for the pool below the canyon. He was vague about it, but pointed on up the logging road.

"How far is it to the end of the road?" Darrah asked.

"Two or three miles," he said. "Maybe four or five. I've never been there."

"How long have you lived in the valley?"

"Fourteen years. Go handlogging. Partner's sick in hospital. Back pretty soon." He sighed heavily and wiped the sweat from his forehead. Then he glanced towards the mountain tops behind us and his face brightened considerably. "There's a gold mine in here," he said. "You know that? Lots of gold. Fellow told me about it long ago. Up there in the draw."

He pointed to a cleft in the mountains.

"Are you working it?" I asked.

"Can't find it. Hard to find. I'll go up there today and look. Four thousand feet up."

"It's pretty hot to climb that far," I said.

He shrugged. "Maybe tomorrow cooler. Find it tomorrow. Then no more work."

We talked a little longer, then went on up the road.

"You think he could make it up to four thousand feet?" I asked Darrah.

"It's an engineering possibility, I suppose, but I wouldn't bet on it. Do you think there's anything in the gold story?"

"There doesn't need to be," I said. "So long as he keeps figuring he'll find it tomorrow. It's kept him going fourteen years."

The road must have been nearer five than three miles long, because it took an hour and thirty-five minutes to reach the end of it from salt water. The river was generally close, often within sight of it, and we fished our way back, trying a pool here and there. For the most part it was a rocky torrent which seemed to offer little good holding water at that height. There was no sign of big fish, either humpback or steelhead, but we caught a few yearling steelheads, so I felt satisfied that the mature fish do pass the canyon successfully.

Below the canyon we fished the big pool. The fly produced nothing at all from the murky water, though a nice fish had rolled within easy reach soon after we arrived there. A favorite devon minnow was equally invisible or else contemptuously disregarded, so I put on a small bright spoon. The fish took it at once and went off with all the brilliant speed of a summer steelhead. We beached her at last—that is to say, we brought her up for the third time before we could persuade her to stay on the rocky slopes that passed for beaches—a slender, silvery female of seven pounds. It seemed enough to show that the river was too heavily silted for the fly, but we felt we had learned a good deal about it for the future.

Almost back to back with the Brem, flowing north into Ramsay Arm instead of south into Toba Inlet, is the Quatham. I had heard it held summer steelhead and hoped it might not be glacial, so we ran to it the next morning. It was clear and very low. At the small logging camp, Mr. Sandberg, the owner, confirmed the idea that steelhead run to the stream—there were several in a small pool where his logging road crossed about five miles up—but told us a forest fire closure had gone into effect the previous evening, which meant we couldn't go up.

By this time we had noticed a school of small herring sheltering under the float we were tied to. Several times a larger fish flashed under them—feeding king salmon, Sandberg said. Then I saw a cutthroat trout of about two pounds hanging briefly in the water a little beyond the edge of the float. It was enough. I went off to the mouth of the river while the others began picking out spoons for the kings.

The stream was small, but had a nice run under a cut bank a few yards up from salt water. A good trout took my fly

almost at once, ran thirty or forty yards jumping steadily
and threw the hook. Peering over the thick brush into a
tiny pool at the next bend I saw a fine big cutthroat, probably nearer four pounds than three. I made some awkward
movements and got a fly over him in some sort of fashion
several times. But presumably he had seen me too, because
he would have nothing to do with it and finally moved
lazily away under a log jam at the head of the pool.

Above there the stream spread out among wide gravel
bars and I knew there was no hope of finding a fish, so I
turned down again to the run under the cut bank. The
first two fish I took from it were Dolly Vardens of about
a pound. Then another cutthroat took, a bright and pretty
fish of two and a half pounds. He fought fast and made
seven clear and splendid jumps before I could bring him
to the beach.

Good though it was, the mouth of the little river didn't
offer much scope. The others had taken a cutthroat or two
off the float, but hadn't been able to stir up the kings, so
we decided again to move on.

The fire closure had pretty well stifled our original plan
to explore likely summer steelhead streams, but we decided
to look in at the mouth of Moh Creek, in Bute Inlet. Darrah
and I went ashore there and found a good stream flowing
out into a big tidal pool through a high, straight-walled
box canyon. It was a pretty place, unspoiled by logging,
with big maples hanging out over the pool, and Sedum and
sea pinks blooming on the rock. Bandtailed pigeons and
hummingbirds were there in force and a lively colony of
rough-winged swallows swept and turned across the surface of the water.

The big pool seemed to promise almost anything at all. Herrings were schooled in good numbers along one side of it, there were needlefish in the eddies and the greenish water hid the secrets of the deeper place. We worked it over with fly and spinner and spoon, but caught only Dolly Vardens about fifteen inches long. A trail that led around the rocks and presumably on upstream above the canyon tempted us. But there was the fire closure and, more compelling perhaps, the fact that we had less than an hour to catch the slack tide in Arran Rapids on our way through to Loughborough Inlet.

By the time we got to Loughborough Inlet and anchored in Sidney Bay we were running a little short of likely places to prospect. But Heydon Creek, which drains a good-sized lake and once had a famous sockeye run, seemed a good possibility. Letcher and I ran up there next morning in the small boat, only to find a large logging camp with log booms completely barring the way upstream. Nothing about it looked very promising, so we turned back.

On the way up, almost opposite our anchorage, I had noticed a wide grass flat backed by a stand of alders, behind two rocky islets. There was a fairly wide valley behind it, so it seemed a likely place to expect a good-sized creek. Letcher agreed it was worth looking into, so we ran there.

The creek was disappointingly small when we found it, just a trickle of water among rocks covered with green algae, but there were signs it ran strongly enough in fall and winter. There was a pleasant breeze across the seagrass meadow, so we sat there and made a good lunch of deviled ham sandwiches, raw onions and beer. The bay in front of us was quite symmetrical, almost a semicircle, and a shallow bar of pale sand and gravel ran in a curve from each point to the rocky islets in the center of the bay. Even without fish, it was a far pleasanter place to be than the cluttered mouth of Heydon Creek.

After lunch I pulled on a pair of waders and began to search the shallows off the creek mouth while Letcher went to bring up the boat. The shallows seemed to me too staringly open under the bright sun, so I was glad enough to climb aboard when Letcher came with the boat. He took my rod and put it in the stern with the others while I pulled off my waders and rowed slowly towards the drop-off. Letcher then picked up his casting rod—we each had a fly rod and a casting rod in the boat—and began to put up a little silver Andy Reeker spoon, which is his favorite machine of search for cutthroat trout in salt water.

The drop-off was pretty—a sharp break into deep green water almost soupy with plankton and flashing with herrings and needlefish. I turned the boat lazily along it. Almost immediately a reel started to run, hard and fast, and the three rods lying beside Letcher began to jump. I recognized the sound easily enough—it was my reel—scrambled across and grabbed up the appropriate rod, which miraculously came free of the others. The fish was still on and still running. He jumped once, then again, about fifty yards behind the boat, and the leader broke. It was a coho salmon of four or five pounds, a little too sudden for 2x gut and the heavy-handed treatment I had given him.

Letcher looked at me reproachfully. "Gosh," he said. "You're careless to leave a fly trailing like that."

"You took it aboard for me," I said. "Remember? I was in the water."

But it isn't every day that a salt-water coho takes a No. 6 fly trailing ten feet behind a boat, and I think we both suspected we were on to something good. We were. Moments later a two-pound cutthroat took the Andy Reeker. I had put up a heavier leader and another fly meanwhile and took another almost as quickly as I could throw it out. Letcher quickly changed to his fly rod and so it went through the sunny afternoon as we worked slowly back and forth along the bar, from the westerly point of the bay to the little islands. The fish were all about the same, either fat, greenbacked cutthroats of two pounds or strong quick coho salmon running from four to six pounds. The tide was running up the inlet, piling the feed against the bar; the herrings and needlefish were hard at work on it and the cohos and cutthroats were hard at work on them. Every trip along the bar hooked us three or four fish, the cohos generally out by the islands, the cutthroats closer inshore, but we never really knew which would take next.

With the sun at our backs, the fish were often plainly visible as they came to the fly in the green water. And they didn't want large flies—No. 4 or 6 was quite good enough. Altogether, it was about as good as salt-water fishing can be, or as any fishing need be. And just to prove it wasn't a one-shot affair, Darrah and I went back next morning, on the ebb tide, and fished the bar between the east point of the bay and the islands.

To be perfectly truthful, the tide down the inlet didn't set quite as well against the bar, the fish were not quite so plentiful, and the tide was a good deal harder to work. Because it was harder to work, we ran the little inboard motor instead of rowing, which explains but does not excuse an entry in the *Wanderer*'s log-book to this effect: "To land a huge grilse of about two pounds, our anglers adopted the unique method of engaging the casting line to the propeller, thus dragging him to the dinghy without effective resistance on his part."

I should like to clarify this matter a little. I hooked the fish in question and was demonstrating to Darrah how quietly a hooked fish will lie if one doesn't apply pressure. During this demonstration the line became involved with the propeller. With great presence of mind I stopped the motor. Since the entangled line was a valued fly line, Darrah went to the bow while I went to the stern, rolled up my sleeves and began the salvage work. Some fifteen profane minutes later the line was free. I then played the fish and brought it safely to the boat. Throughout the entire salvage operation the hooked fish had remained perfectly quiet, a convincing if unplanned demonstration. And it weighed four pounds, not two.

2. *The Beaches*

GIVEN THE RIGHT CONDITIONS OF HIGH tide and calm water, small herrings occasionally pack in against the beaches along the east coast of Vancouver Island and hold there for several days at a time. In June and July the cohos and smaller kings feeding in the Gulf of Georgia find them and drive in to the attack. It can make some very unusual and worthwhile fishing.

A good number of coho salmon live out their whole salt-water life in the broad reaches of the Gulf of Georgia and the nearby inlets. They come down from their streams after a year of aggressive fresh-water feeding— they are the most aggressive of all the salmon and trouts in their pre-migrant stage—and quickly put their activity and determination to good use amid the new abundance; by February or March of the following year they weigh almost two pounds; by the end of May probably three pounds; by July five or six pounds; and in October they are fully mature fish of eight or ten pounds, ready to go up the rivers to spawn and die.

From the size of ten or twelve inches up to two or three pounds, the young fish are popularly called "grilse" and are heavily attacked by anglers, who kill at least a quarter of a million of them a year. This represents a fantastic waste, because the survival rate of active young fish of this size would otherwise be extremely high; and it probably accounts to some extent for the great deterioration of coho fishing in the Gulf of Georgia during the past ten or twenty years. It is true that other and more important factors are also involved, but sportsmen could ensure themselves a lot more sport merely by insisting on a three-pound limit.

From three pounds up—and this is still the commercial limit on these fish—the coho is one of the finest game fish there are. At four, five and six pounds, which are the usual weights of fish caught along the beaches in the summer months, they can run a hundred yards or more on the right tackle and often jump several times.

There are several ways of beach fishing. Given a decent abundance of fish, or a particularly likely spot with some tide running, the fly is good enough—a heavily dressed polar bear wing with a silver body on a No. 1 hook does very well. But fish follow the fly a long way instead of striking promptly as they do at a spinner, so it is better to go hunting for them with a spinning or casting rod. Any one of a hundred lures can be effective, but one of the best is the narrow Gresvig crocodile spinner, which is also heavy enough to cast well.

One of my favorite hunting places is the south point of Menzies Bay. One can turn in either direction—back into the bay along a succession of shingle beaches until the rock bluffs begin near the old camp, or southward towards Race Point, which is all rock and fairly easy traveling once one is past the first bay. Except at the short periods of slack, the tide is always running strongly, sometimes very strongly, past the points, and eddying into the bays.

I usually start out with the hope that I am going to find acres of herrings or needlefish packed close against the

shore and salmon slashing and driving everywhere amongst
them. This could happen, but almost never does. Rather it
is a matter of enjoying what is there—the lively water, the
familiar shapes of the nearby hills, the distant mountains,
the cloud formations, the rustle of wind in the dry grasses
that grow in the rock clefts. The fish that come most commonly to the spinner will be rockfish, either copper- or
yellow-striped. They are easily released if one has a pair of
pliers or make admirable fillets if one feels inclined to kill
them. Sometimes there are blue-green cutthroat trout inside
the kelp beds, far more beautiful than any river fish, or
Dolly Vardens with a lucent overlay of turquoise on spots
and fins and back. Sometimes a coho or a feeding king
strikes hard, tears off line and comes to beach; then the
whole day has a glow of success about it.

But fish or no, there will always be excitements. Sometimes there will be salmon jumping or feeding just beyond
casting reach, so one casts and casts with the conviction
that there must be others closer in or else that these same
unattainable ones will move into range. Sometimes the deep
water out from the foot of the rocks is speckled all through
with the flashes of feeding herrings. Then it seems certain
that salmon are somewhere close under them, bound to
turn up to the first winking traverse of the spoon. Just for
good measure I assume that the imagined fish are enormous
kings of forty pounds and upwards, which they well might
be but never have been in my experience; if any salmon at
all comes, it is usually a modest six- or eight-pounder.

The rest of the day is made up of many things. Ospreys
and bald eagles fight their battles over the water, seals and
sometimes otters are at their own fishing. Kingfishers scold

and dive, a heron takes up his measured dignity of flight or
sweeps to a landing on some favorite beach, gulls and
murrelets, cormorants, mergansers and scoters all have their
affairs with the fish. Sandpipers start from the beaches or
wheel out over the water to settle and feed on the tide rips.
Porpoises may roll nearby or the killer whales pass in stately
procession. Underfoot the little green crabs come out to
feed as the tide works up among the rocks, hermit crabs
stalk along the bottom, sandhoppers swim off, some swiftly
and purposefully under water, some circling aimlessly on
the surface. Very well worth watching are the sandhoppers.
There are many kinds and many colors, brown and blue
and pink and orange; they can jump or burrow or walk or
swim—the first three of these things equally well on land
or under water. I once watched one swim to a submerged
rock, walk across it, jump through the water to an exposed
rock, jump from there to a drifting alder leaf, walk easily
across that and finally swim down out of sight.

And it is in this sort of thing rather than the fishing itself
that the real pleasures of hunting salmon along the beaches
really lie.

It is far more productive to go to some point or bar where
the salmon regularly come in, wade out and keep fishing
through an evening or a tidal stage. Two friends of mine,
Charlie de Feo and Meade Schaeffer, had still another solution, though perhaps a rather specialized one. Being artists
as well as fishermen they took their painting and their fly
rods to the more likely beaches. There they would set up
rods and easels, pull on waders and go to work with ears
cocked for the splash of a feeding fish and eyes ready to
mark the swirl. When the splash came and the swirl was

spotted one or both would drop brushes, grab fly rods and run.

In the evenings Charlie, who is one of the world's better fly-tiers, would apply his ingenuity and his wonderful collection of materials to creating more and more beautiful patterns that would give keener hope to the next day's painting. In total and in spite of frequent interruptions, I think more paintings were painted than fish were caught. But I found them one evening busily painting, each with a fresh-caught nine-pound king beside his easel. Moments later they were both in the water and Charlie was yelling in triumph as a coho ran and jumped with his fly.

The truth is that one might happen on to a spectacular flurry of inshore feeding either by walking the beaches or by waiting at a likely place, but either one is a long chance. The surest way to good beach fishing is when the word comes that the "herrings were in last night" at one of the well-known beaches, and the salmon were hard after them.

Then it is a small *fiesta*. Everyone goes, with children, babies, dogs, supper and enthusiasm. We have a beach of this sort a little way south of Campbell River. On a good tide in July the herrings will pack tight all along it and in the evenings the salmon come after them. Wade out ten feet into the water and as likely as not there will be a flurry of feeding cohos between you and the shore, with herrings jumping out in the evening light and the bulges and swirls of the salmon showing under them.

It is a question whether it is more fun to watch or to fish. I usually settle for 10 per cent fishing, 90 per cent watching and gossiping. So much will be happening and so many friends will be there that to fish is to miss altogether too

much. I think of Don Marshall, standing knee-deep in the
water, pitching out his spoon and bringing it back, in that
calm, easy, graceful way he has with everything, from a
baseball glove to a shotgun. He struck at a pull, felt nothing
and went on reeling.

"That's six," he said. "And missed every one. Last night
I only had four strikes and hooked every one solid."

His wife, standing on the beach behind him, said: "Perhaps I'd better take it now, dear."

Don laughed and handed her the rod. She threw the
spoon out, immediately hooked a fish, lost it, threw it out
again and hooked another. Don's small daughter saw the
action, came running up, threw her spoon beside her
mother's fish and hooked yet another. Don sat on a log
and watched his women play the fish he couldn't hook.

Fifteen or twenty feet away Hank Davis had a fish that
was heading out for the middle of the Gulf. Just beyond
him a woman grew impatient with the friction drive of her
spinning reel, threw her rod down and began handlining
six-pound monofilament. Her husband protested mildly behind her, but the fish was coming in fast now, splashing
and floundering at the surface. Three or four feet from the
beach it broke the line.

The lady looked reproachfully at her husband. "It's that
line again," she said. "I told you it was no good. You'll
have to do something about it."

There was a surge of wild feeding farther up the beach.
Half the baseball team came thundering by as though heading collectively for first base on a poorly placed bunt. The
beach was pretty well crowded now, with a man, woman
or child plopping out a spoon every fifteen or twenty feet

along it. Smaller children and dogs ran up and down the
logs. "Daddy's got one." "He's lost it." "He's got another."
It was quite an evening. The Marshall family finished up
with five good fish between them; Ty Conti had five and
his wife two more. Hank had two or three. Hector from
the welding shop had two and had lost a dozen more, two
of them with spoons; one quiet young man said neither he
nor his wife had ever fished before, but they thought it was
pretty good sport and they might stay with it—they had six
silvery five-pounders between them.

The cohos slowed a little, but the dogfish moved in and
began taking spoons and herrings in their place, which
made for squeals and excitement. Then it was dusk and a
great red moon began to climb slowly over the water. The
evening was over.

All in all, there's a lot to be said for the beaches. They
can give you everything from the extremes of solitude to
the gayest of parties and sometimes a few fish to remember
as well.

3. *Stream Survival*

ALL SORTS OF THEORIES HAVE BEEN AD-
vanced to account for the fact that salmon and large migratory trout, though not feeding, frequently take flies and
lures and bait in fresh water. I have long been satisfied that
they do so because the lure stimulates the conditioned reflex
to chase and seize it that has become only partially dormant
in the sexual changes of maturity.

At this point another interesting question comes up: is it
the salt-water feeding reflex that is triggered, or do the fish
revert partially to the conditioning of their fresh-water
years? From the wide variation of lures that is taken—all
the way from great flashing spoons to tiny flies—I am inclined to think that both types of reflex are there and either
can be tripped, at least under some conditions and in certain
individuals. But at the same time it is altogether likely that
the conditioning of the fresh-water years plays the greater
part.

The reason I say this is because the fish that most readily
take in fresh water are those with the longest fresh-water
life histories and those closest to their fresh-water life.

Consider first the Pacific salmon. The humpback goes to
sea as soon as he is free-swimming and has no fresh-water
feeding life. A good run of humpbacks comes into the
Campbell. I have fished over thousands of them, year after
year, yet have hooked only one, a spawned-out male, on

the fly. I have taken a few, very few, on spinning lures of one sort or another, and have seen a very few taken by other anglers in the same way. For some strange reason humpbacks in the Oyster, a river only thirteen miles away, take so freely in some years that they are a nuisance, but so far as I know this is only after they have started to spawn, when other factors enter.

The dog salmon, like the humpback, has practically no fresh-water life before going to sea. I have fished over rivers that were practically solid with them and while I have taken a few on spoons and spinners, it has never been easy. One can safely say that neither the dog nor the humpback take readily enough in fresh water to make fishing for them worthwhile.

The sockeye is a law to itself. It may have one, two or even three years of fresh-water feeding, but these are spent in lakes, not streams, and the feed is minute forms of plankton which are impossible to imitate. The sockeye does not return to the lake of its youth, except in passing, so the conditions of its fresh-water feeding environment are not repeated. Even so, sockeyes take the fly very readily at certain places in some streams—the Brooks River in Alaska is a notable example, and the chances are that the Brooks River sockeye have a fresh-water life of two, if not three, years.

The king salmon normally spends a few weeks in fresh-water feeding before running to sea, though a certain number of them, perhaps as many as 20 per cent in some rivers, may feed in fresh water for a full year. King salmon will take lures and spoons in fresh water fairly readily. I fish my flies over hundreds of them every season, but I am sure of only one that came to the fly before he had moved to the shallows to begin spawning. Once they are spread on the shallows they may take a fly as small as No. 6 fairly readily. King salmon "jacks"—that is males maturing to spawn after only one year in salt water—take much more readily.

The coho salmon spends one full year in fresh-water feeding, usually in a stream. He is an aggressive and extremely active little fish. He spends only two years in salt water and on his return to the stream will take fly or spinner quite readily. I have even taken one coho on a floating fly. Coho jacks take even more freely than king salmon jacks, or perhaps there are just more of them.

That seems to complete the case pretty firmly so far as Pacific salmon are concerned. The longer their stay in fresh water, the shorter their stay in salt water after that, the more likely they are to take on their final return to fresh water. But the case seems to hold equally well for steelhead and Atlantic salmon.

Both these fish normally spend two years in fresh water, usually in streams. Both return for the first time after two years of sea-feeding. Both will readily take dry and wet flies, spoons, spinners and bait. Winter fish of both species are harder to move than summer fish, but this is of no significance because the lethargy of the fish at winter water temperatures readily accounts for it. Both Atlantic salmon and steelhead grilse take very freely indeed.

This argument seems to me of considerable importance to the angler in suggesting which fish to go after and how best to go after them. But it is of even greater importance in emphasizing the absolutely fundamental part played by streams in the raising of the better game fish.

Fishermen far too often think of streams only in terms of spawning. Can the fish get up them? Are the spawning areas adequate? Is the water clean and good? All these points are absolutely essential, but they are only part of the story.

A stream's capacity to raise sea-going migrants from Atlantic salmon, steelhead, coho and even king salmon eggs is rigidly limited by its food supply. This in turn is related to such matters as the mineral content of the water, the type and quality of the bottom, weed growth, shelter, temperature, rate of flow and other such things that it may or may not be easy to control. But in most streams the first limiting factor is the minimum summer flow. At this point the carrying capacity of the stream is very much less than during the abundance of spring and winter flows; the young fish are in crowded competition and great numbers literally starve to death. Dr. Ferris Neave showed that the return of coho salmon to the Cowichan River on Vancouver Island in the years from 1940 to 1947 almost exactly reflected the minimum summer flow of the river two years previously.* He has also pointed out that "British Columbia streams do not usually produce more than twenty sea-going coho smolts per hundred square yards of accessible stream area."

Nearly all our coho and steelhead streams have suffered major reductions of summer flow through clear logging and burning over the past fifty years. In many of these streams the flows are, or should be, improving through the regrowth of ground-cover. But dozens of them could be still further

* Ferris Neave, et al. *The Investigation of Fish-Power Problems.* (Institute of Fisheries, University of British Columbia. Vancouver, 1958.)

improved by building small retaining dams from which extra water could be fed into the streams during periods of low flow.

Work of this kind, which need not cost very much, would be a big first step in building back the runs. And there is no need to stop there. With modern machinery it should not be either difficult or expensive to improve many of the physical characteristics of the streams themselves so that they would have a greater capacity for raising migrants. Beyond this again, if spawning proved to be inadequate to stock the stream's new capacity, it would be a simple matter to improve spawning areas or even to create artificial ones, as was so successfully done for humpback salmon at Jones Creek.

I think of this as "gardening" the rearing streams and I am sure we shall come to it in the end. I only wish it could be soon rather than late, because the possibilities seem to me so sharply exciting. The work would have to be undertaken gradually, over many seasons, and no doubt there would be problems and expense in maintaining it. But the results on each stream would be wholesale, not patchwork and piecemeal like the expensive rearing and stocking programs that produce so little effect. Migrants, whether steelheads or cutthroats or Pacific salmons, will always provide most of the best fishing up and down the Pacific Coast. We are a long way from using the capacity of the ocean to grow smolts to adult fish, but if we would help the fry grow into smolts we might go a little way towards testing it.

PART SEVEN

Return to the River

1. *Nimpkish River*

THE NIMPKISH WAS THE FIRST NORTH American river that I felt I had in some measure made my own. I fished it a lot in the late twenties and early thirties, trapped and hunted and camped along its banks, traveled it by canoe and skiff and once even in a home-made scow. I had been upset in it, half-drowned in it and considerably scared by it more than once. I had seen it in the fury of full freshet, in the ice-bound attrition of winter and in the comparative gentleness of summer. I had watched its great salmon runs with ever-increasing wonder. In it I had caught cutthroats and steelheads and, by fair means and foul, all five species of Pacific salmon. Above all, I had first learned there to catch the big king salmon, sachems as the Indians called them, tyees to the sportsman.

In 1933 I left the river and though living within a hundred miles of it, I did not get back for over twenty years. I had been busy and so had my partner of the Nimpkish years, Ed Lansdowne. We had married, fathered children and settled down. And there had been a war and the matter of sorting things out again after a war. So when we came together again on the Nimpkish in late August of 1955, my son Alan was thirteen and Ed's Donny and David were only a little younger.

Ed had a new canoe, fifteen feet long, bright scarlet, quick and light as a feather. It was hot, bright weather and the boys, especially Alan who was the stranger, wanted to see everything—Cheslakees, the terraced site of the original Indian village, the hulk of the *Chakawana* where we had dragged her up behind the Indian Island in 1932, the burial trees by the slough, the burial caves above the first rapid. That first day we did not care too much about fishing, which was probably just as well, because the river was dead low and the seals were working up as far as Ned's Canyon.

The river was little changed after twenty years. Eustace Hill, where I had killed the big buck with a twenty-two and Ed had shot a bear with the same rifle, was logged; but it was hardly noticeable as change. The tyees were still finning in the tidal water and rolling in the first pool. Above the first rapid the canyon was the same and beyond there the timber still stood untouched, big spruce and hemlock and Douglas fir. Ned's smokehouses were snow-flattened at the foot of his canyon and a jungle of salmonberries and giant nettles discouraged Alan from exploring the ruins.

Triangle rapids still made a recognizable triangle of rocks and the heavy run where the big cutthroats sometimes lie is still beside them, under the right bank.

But the river was low, dead low, lower than I had ever seen it. "That's the way it is in summer now," Ed told me. "I guess it's all the logging around Woss Lake and up the Kla-anche Valley."

We had to carry the canoe over Otter Island to get past Wright's Camp. The rocky bones of the rapids showed plainly. The three fierce backward-curling waves in front of Wright's Camp were only a foaming pool. The sharp break on the return bend below, sliding against Siwash Rock and the entrance to the canyon, was now a little fall, clearly marked across the width of the river. Rocks and boulders had piled in against the upstream side of Siwash Rock itself and I found myself wading there no more than hip-deep. Buried somewhere under my feet, I knew, were a Hudson's Bay ax, a 25-20 rifle of fabulous accuracy and two dozen traps—dumped when Ed and I rolled our canoe in the cold winter of 1931-2.

We found a few trout, but only a few, which was not surprising with the low water and bright sun and the over-friendly seals. In the tidal water I tried briefly to get a spoon across one of the schools of finning tyees, but the flood tide was bringing the green weed thickly into the river and it was a discouraging business. Besides, it didn't really matter; tomorrow was another day and tomorrow, I told the boys, it would be time for a little serious fishing.

The tyees at Nimpkish are like tyees everywhere, by no means easy to persuade. They can be taken in the salt water off the mouth of the river, out as far as Green Island and down as far as Theimar Creek; when a fresh run is in, they take there almost freely. They will strike at times inside the river mouth, anywhere from the deep water off Cheslakees village right up to the first pool below the canyon which we call Lansdowne Pool. I like this pool best of all, even though it is probably the hardest place to take a fish, because it is really a fresh-water pool; all but the smallest tides reach up to it, but the river influence is too strong for weed or other tidal drift and the fresh water keeps out all tidal water growth.

Lansdowne Pool is big and wide and deep, with good runs of current below the rapid at the head, gathering to a firm even flow along the solid rock of the left bank, right out to the tail of the pool. The big fish lie there in great numbers, waiting to go on up the river on the first rise. Generally it is possible to hook one, perhaps even two, after the sun has gone off the pool; but Ed and I have never forgotten a day in 1932 when we started hooking fish at three in the afternoon and kept hooking them, monster after monster, until dark. It had never happened before and it has never happened since, but there isn't a reason in the world why it couldn't.

The boys had more exploring to do next day and it was three in the afternoon before I began fishing the pool. I have never felt more confident. Fish were rolling everywhere. I had twenty years of experience behind me since those older times and the canoe was full of plugs and flat-fish and other lures we had never dreamed of in our years of innocence. The Nimpkish tyees, I felt, were due for a great surprise and it was going to be a real pleasure to surprise them.

Ed had rigged an anchor on a long rope and was able to drop me back at regular intervals between casts, so that I could be sure of covering the water. I had a four-inch silex reel with two hundred yards of eighteen-pound line and a Hardy Murdoch rod that would get the heavy plugs and spoons well out across the holding water. And the plugs were of the most up-to-date and efficient design, in a range of wonderfully seductive colors. Even if it were not another great afternoon like that one in 1932, I felt I could surely count on more lively action than we had ever been able to stir on ordinary afternoons.

The plugs looked good in the water and I worked them hard. Huge fish rolled right in the line of their swing, rolled behind them, in front of them and on both sides of them. But nothing happened. I changed plugs, I put on more lead, we swung the canoe over to a better position, and still nothing happened. The boys had been fishing for trout in the rapid above us, but had now wandered off to the burial caves again. Ed and I looked at each other.

"We've talked so much about it," Ed said. "We've got to produce for them somehow."

"What do you think of those plugs?" I asked him.

"They look good. They catch fish in the salt chuck."

I had lost faith. "I don't like the damn things," I said. "They jump all over the place. Can't tell whether they're fishing near bottom or six feet off."

"You've been bumping the lead on bottom."

"I know. But what happens a few seconds later?"

"Why don't you try a spoon, then?"

I tried spoons. Not those old-fashioned things we had

used twenty years ago, but modern improved spoons. Still nothing happened.

"Better go and check on the boys," I told Ed. "Maybe we'll have to wait till the sun gets behind the hill." It was a cloudy day, but I had to say something.

"Giving up?" Ed asked me, knowing I wasn't.

"Hell, no," I said. "Put me off over on the far side. I'll do it from my feet."

I was glad of the solid ground. A canoe or a boat is fine— sometimes it is the only way—but from one's feet one can really fish; there is no wondering whether the canoe has swung or drifted, no question about how far one has moved down between casts; one can search with precision and make sure of covering what should be covered.

And I was finished with the new-fangled plugs and spoons. Maybe they had something, but another day would do for experiments; today I wanted to catch a fish. In a little velvet pouch I had a set of the original spoons, the ones we had started with, discarded and turned back to after many trials and experiments—"Superior" is the maker's name for them, "Washboards" the commercial trollers used to call them. Mine were No. 6's, four and a half inches long by about one and a half wide, copper, silver and brass, mounted with flat-sided Allcock single hooks. I chose the copper, because it had always done best for us in the pool, and began fishing.

Ahead of me was two or three hundred feet of solid rock bank, slippery in places and sloping awkwardly, sometimes too close to the bush and complicated by a large, stranded boomstick at the far end. On the low river the current was pretty well smoothed out by the time it turned along the rock, but flowing fast enough to make for a nice swing on each cast and bring the spoon slowly and evenly into the deep water. The Superior is a light spoon and difficult to cast well unless it goes out on edge against the air resistance, but that day it was going out on edge for me and I was reaching just about wherever I wanted.

No fish were showing over the deep water under the bank; they rarely do show there, but they lie there and usually they take better there than in the livelier and shallower water. Even so, it was a temptation to throw at every fish that rolled in the shallower water across the pool, and I did not resist the temptation. How could I? They were beautiful, huge and hog-backed and lazy, not even bronzed by the fresh water as yet, infinitely desirable—and, it began to seem, quite unattainable.

I covered fish after rolling fish, exactly as I wanted to. I brought the spoon across them, behind them, right over them, even downstream at them. Once I felt a solid stop in midstream, struck hard at it and felt nothing more. It was a fish all right, but I knew it would take more than that to impress the boys.

I saw them coming back down the rapid with Ed, two or three hundred yards away. I didn't know until he told me later that Alan was saying: "Let's go down and pick him up. He's never going to catch a fish now," or that Ed was answering him: "Better not sell your old man short; I've seen him work a whole lot longer than that and come up with a fish."

But I did know that my time was running out and so was the good water ahead of me. And I suddenly realized that within the next two or three casts I would be covering

exactly the place where the very first tyee had taken me in
the pool. I cast again, a good long swing clear over to the
shallows and a little below me. I picked it up fast at first to
keep it just off the rocks, then let it settle into the deeper
part of the pool. It was a beautiful sweep, smooth and easy,
just fast enough to keep the spoon working, slow enough
to let it well down, but no different from a hundred others
I had made that afternoon. The fish took just over on my
side of midstream, and I hit him hard.

He was slow about taking off, as they often are. Just to
make sure the hook was really home I hit him again, two
or three times, with all the line would stand, before I yelled.
He started off majestically, then faster and faster, diag-
onally down and across the pool. In the shallows he broke
in a flurry, then calmed down and came back, keeping well
over. I was just as glad, because I would have had to swim
to follow him.

Opposite me he made two quiet rolls and kept going. All
the pressure I could put on him made not the slightest difference. He simply took line, slowly, inevitably, with an
absolute power that brought back a flood of good memories.
As he rolled I had judged him not over forty pounds, but
now I began to wonder. He was in good safe water, traveling in a good safe direction, but not nearly fast enough for
my liking. Neither the force of the current nor his own
speed was enough to take much strength out of him.

A little way below the rapid he turned of his own accord
and came slowly back to the deep water in front of me.
By this time Ed and the boys had come over with the canoe
and were holding beside the rock just upstream. That gave
me a little more security, so I shook him up and he ran

again, hard downstream and broke nicely two or three times.

"Do you want to come into the canoe?" Ed asked.

"I'd better get a bit more steam out of him first, maybe." I thought two large men, three boys and a lively forty-pounder might be an upsetting combination in a fifteen-foot canoe, in spite of Ed's expertness. I brought the fish back and he ran again, still strong. When he came back from that I began to size up the prospects of gaffing him from the beach. They weren't good. It was a straight drop-off into deep water all the way along. Besides, there was the boom-stick, unless I could work upstream quite a bit. There wasn't room to stand and gaff him outside it and it would be quite a trick to reach out over it, even without the matter of lifting him across it on the gaff. I decided the canoe was the right idea.

Ed and the boys brought it nicely alongside. I scrambled over the boomstick somehow and got in just as the fish started on another run. He was still majestic and powerful and we all cheered as he surged out twice over the shallows on the far side.

"Where'll we get him?" Ed asked.

"The Blue Clay if he makes up his mind to go," I said. "But I'd rather try it at Mather's place." Mather's was a fair rocky beach three or four hundred yards down from us.

But the fish came back tired. He saw the canoe, decided it was welcome shelter, swam under and stayed there. The small rapid below us was rocky and very shallow now that the tide had ebbed.

"Better ease over to dry land," I said. "I'll try and get him from that grassy place at the tail of the pool."

"Could reach under the canoe and gaff him," Donny suggested.

"No," I said. "By the time we'd picked ourselves up off the rocks he'd be gone."

The fish stayed with us, as closely as he could under the canoe all the way to the grassy place. He was tired, but rolling in the way that sometimes shakes a hook loose. I was glad to jump ashore and get him clear of the canoe. Ed gaffed him for me—thirty-seven pounds, forty-two inches long; a handsome fish, clean and bright and thick.

I owed him a lot. Nothing had happened just the way I had imagined it would, but only because I hadn't the imagination to think up anything so completely appropriate. The copper Superior spoon is back in its velvet pouch, waiting for another time that will come quite soon now. It takes fish in the pool as nothing else will. At the same time, I can't help wondering what a good big Gresvig crocodile spoon might do. It would cast a lot better. And the faster action. . . . So far as that goes I'm still not satisfied I can't make those big fish in the pool take a fly.

2. *Tsable River*

MY FRIEND DUNC MARSHALL IS A MA-
chinist by trade and a good one. He is also a good fisherman
and a first-rate wing shot. Until recently he was a peppery
baseball player and though he has assumed a great measure
of dignity with the passing years and become a manager,
he can still find picturesque phrases directed towards the
mental or moral improvement of a careless umpire or an
aggressive opponent. With these virtues, added to a number
of others I haven't time to describe at the moment, Dunc
shapes up as one of the liveliest and most satisfying friends
and companions I have. There is no one I would rather be
out with.

Dunc was born and raised in a small coal-mining town on
the east coast of Vancouver Island, called Union Bay,
which gives him still another asset I admire and envy—a
British Columbia childhood. It was a particularly good
childhood because Union Bay, like many coal-mining
towns, had a population made up chiefly of sportsmen—
miners, machinists, trainmen and others who, when they
weren't chasing soccer balls or baseballs, were just as busily
chasing game or fish. They were both good and keen, these
men, with a strong flavoring of old country tradition and
ethics. And in the twenties and early thirties, when Dunc
began to use guns and rifles and rods, it was a good time
for a young fellow to learn from them because there weren't

too many people around and fish and game were plentiful. The brant flew faithfully to Seal Island and Denman Island and Comox Spit; deer and blue grouse were abundant in the new logging slashes; ruffed grouse haunted the swamp edges and the grades; there were plenty of salmon in the salt water and steelheads and cutthroats in every creek.

Every so often, Dunc digs into this not-so-distant past and comes up with something that has immediate application. He did so when I saw him early last year. "Gump and I went into the old drill cabins on the Tsable New Year's Day," he told me. "Still standing and still look good, but they were old when I first saw them in 1924."

I vaguely remembered having heard Dunc talk before of good trout fishing in the Tsable, so I asked: "What about the drill cabins?"

"That's where we used to go and stay when we were kids. Finest cutthroats I ever saw anywhere in that creek, cold and hard and perfect, green backs and silver bellies. Fourteen, sixteen inches, up to eighteen or a little better. It's only about fifteen minutes from the drill cabins to the falls pool. We'd go in there and fish down about five miles to salt water, wading the creek. But you can't stay in it. Straight off the ice. Colder than Aunt Fanny's feet, my uncle used to say."

"Did you drive into the drill cabins?"

"Sure. Road's good. The creek was running high. But I've never seen anything like it for clear when the water's down. So clear you could see the trout on the bottom ten or twenty feet down, only you'd have to look for the shadow of the fish first and find it from that. There were some good fishermen fished it those days. Ray Glover for one, though he didn't use a fly much then." I knew by that he already knew what I was thinking. "Andy Stasik, the high-rigger—you must have known him. He was another. Andy was rich enough to buy salmon eggs by the bottle. He'd throw in a whole bottle to bait a pool. We didn't have eggs, just worms. And if we could get hold of a Red-loop leader, Padron Two I think they called them, that was the business. We were really equipped then. Hugh Glover lent us one one day and I lost it in a fish. I knew that meant a kick in the pants, but darned if we didn't get the same fish and the leader back that same day."

"How long since you last fished it?"

"Oh, a long time." He thought a moment. "Not since I was married, that's sure. When would it be? I remember I was playing a lot of baseball at the time. Every Sunday. Around 1934, maybe. Mother was always getting after me, why didn't I go fishing any more. So one Sunday I went. Not far up. Not nearly to the falls."

"You mean you went in from the road bridge? Upstream?"

"That's right. It was all virgin timber then and there was this little rocky pool under a steep sidehill. I hooked a good fish right away, soon as I threw into it. There I was, hanging on to him and the buck came down on the other side of the river. He was a big one, with his horns in the velvet. I don't think he saw me, but something had scared him and he went right into the pool and swam across. And there I was with the buck and the trout swimming around in the same pool."

"What makes you think those fish aren't still there?"

"Come to think of it, I guess they could be. But it's all logged now. Likely the river's changed."

"It still runs clear," I said. "And if it came straight off the ice then, it still does. Even with the timber off it won't have warmed up very much. Why don't we try it sometime?"

"I'd like to. But they never did much there with a fly. None of them tried it. The fish'd see you. We used to pitch in a worm and leave it lay till a fish swam up and took it."

"Dry fly," I said. "Upstream. It'd work. What time did the fish start in?" They were sea-runs, of course.

"Around July first, I guess. Not much before."

"All right," I said. "It's a date. Soon as we can make it after July first."

That turned out to be July fifteenth, one of the hottest days in one of the hottest summers I remember. And a short day, too, because Dunc was taking delivery of a new car and leaving for the interior with his family that evening; it had to be that evening if he was to get off the Island, because of an impending ferry strike.

The stream was just as clear as he remembered it, but it was badly shrunken by the drought and it was warmer than he remembered—around 64 degrees. I thought at first that might not matter very much. The stream flowed through a deep, narrow gully whose steep banks had turned back the logging—from the stream bed itself one could hardly tell there had been any logging. But in spite of this the pools were so small and so open that the high sun reached into every part of them and, not surprisingly, there wasn't a fish to be seen.

It was a lovely stream though, running over pale boulders

and smooth white sandstone slabs, its bottom almost covered in many places by the crawling cases of sedge larvae. Another foot of water, even six inches, would have made an enormous difference in shelter and protection, and I could easily imagine it holding fish in good numbers. There were places, even at this stage of water, where fish might have been hiding under cutbanks, behind big boulders or under the occasional small log jams, but until we came to the Big Pool there was no place in the body of the stream where a sensible fish would expose himself or very long endure the glare of the sun.

The Big Pool is on a sharp bend, close under a steep shale cliff, and parts of it were shaded by the cliff and the timber on top of it. The body of the pool is very deep and strewn with big boulders. Dunc and I climbed on to a shoulder of the cliff, fifteen or twenty feet above the water, and looked down.

"You can see this is it," Dunc said. "The big spot the kids all hit for. Tracks and worm cans strewn from hell to high water."

"If they aren't here, they aren't anywhere," I said.

We began to see them then, first one, then another, five nice fish of fourteen or fifteen inches all down in the deepest place. But they were moving, not hiding. Very slowly they worked up, out over a sandy flat, then round and down to the shelter of the big boulders again. The surface of the pool was glassy smooth with only an imperceptible draw of current over it.

"Well, there they are," Dunc said. "Not very big and not very many, but at least they're fish. What a hope with a fly."

"I don't know," I said. "At least they're moving around. Might bring one up."

"Go give it a try," Dunc said. "I'll watch."

I was already putting up the fly I wanted—one of Charlie de Feo's beautiful pale spiders on a No. 14 hook, with a 5x nylon leader I could hardly see myself. I went down to the bottom of the pool and began to pitch it up, waiting out the slow drifts as best I could, helping them occasionally with a little artificial movement. Dunc kept me posted on the movements of the fish and their interest, which was slight but perceptible. At about the twentieth cast a fish came up fast and took the fly; I felt him hard, but he wasn't hooked.

"That was it," Dunc said. "He had it. You turned him right over. Too bad."

"It might stir up the others," I suggested, hoping hard. "Or it might put them off."

But it wasn't really the time for that sort of fishing. We had only a short day and we wanted to get some exploring done while we were at it. After a few more casts we went on.

There were several nice runs under cutbanks, all too open and shallow now, then two or three fish behind an upturned stump with some drift piled against it, but they saw us as soon as we saw them and quietly withdrew under the stump after a few floats of the fly.

Dunc was wondering about the Borehole and the Falls. He didn't think we had time to make it to the Falls, but thought we should come to the Borehole almost any time.

"We used to come down there off the hill from the road," he said. "The Borehole was at the bottom of the slope and of course the first thing we had to do was put a light to it. Coal gas, I guess. Went up with a big whoosh. But there was a dandy pool right by it."

We came to a long pool of good depth and with a scattering of boulders that looked like fair shelter. But it was easy to see almost anywhere in it and there were no fish. Just above, the river was gathered tightly against the right bank and the water ran down with a good lively bounce for twenty or thirty yards to the head of the pool. The river had turned at a sharp angle and this quick water was shaded from the sun. I left Dunc fishing it and went on up. He joined me shortly.

"I got a rise in that run," he said. "Seemed like a good fish, but he wouldn't come again. You know, that big pool is the Borehole Pool. It's got to be. The Borehole ought to be somewhere around in here."

We looked and couldn't find it, nor the road they had come down from. "Wish Gump was here," Dunc said. "He'd know about it. I'm sure this is the place."

Later we did ask Gump and Gump said there had been a slide which had taken out the road and buried the Borehole. So we knew we had explored the river only to a few hundred yards above the Borehole before turning back.

On the way out we were hurrying a bit to keep Dunc's appointment with the new station wagon. But he told me to try for the fish he had missed. It came at once and shot back downstream in the swift water as soon as I hooked it. I handlined fast, throwing the recovery in the water at my feet. The fish wasn't big—certainly no more than fourteen inches—but it was very strong and fast. I steered it over to where Dunc was sitting on the bank, a little below me, so that he could get a look at it. Just for a second or two it darted back and forth in the shallows, then it shot off into the Borehole Pool. The rod pulled down hard and the leader broke.

"What did you do that for?" Dunc said. "He was worth keeping."

"I didn't do it," I told him. "He did. I was standing on the line."

"That makes it 100 per cent, then. We sure haven't got much to show for ourselves."

But we had. For me a new stream and a good one. For Dunc an old favorite repossessed and proved still worthwhile. Next season we'll go up there a week or two earlier and take a whole day to it. The stream will be running a foot higher and several degrees cooler. If we don't pick up half-a-dozen good fish apiece and make a bigger day of it than the best of those worm and Red-loop leader days, I'll be surprised. And if Gump or one of the Glover boys or Andy Stasik himself is along it will be all the better.

3. *The Beaverkill*

I HAVE NEVER RETURNED TO THE BEAVER-kill, though I shall. I have been there only once in my life, but that once felt like a return, as I think it must to any North American fly-fisherman. For this, after all, is the true cradle of the sport on our continent. We have all heard of it and read of it, and we all owe a great deal to the men who have fished it and to some who fish it still—to Theodore Gordon, Louis Rhead, Edward Hewitt, George La Branche, Jack Atherton and Sparse Grey Hackle, to name only a few of them.

It is a little stream, dancing brightly out of the timbered Catskills in New York State to its junction with the Willowemoc at Roscoe. From the Junction on it is a big stream, but still a trout stream, a stream a man can cast across and wade around in comfort; and it flows through pleasant farm lands. It is heavily fished, I suppose—it must be, with a name so famous in a state so populous. It is artificially stocked each year with tiny fish. It has largely lost its brook trout, and most of the introduced rainbows that Theodore Gordon wondered about and finally approved of. But the European brown trout is there and in charge. Some of the little fish spawned by the hatchery trucks or planted by the clubs of the upper river manage to evade anglers and survive the heat of summer and the ice of winter. Hold-overs, wise and cautious, they may well survive another season and another, to become fish of minor legend and make worthwhile sport for the faithful who try from "fine and far off."

I may as well admit I have never really fished the Beaver-kill. But I was there on opening day a year or two back with Ed Zern of *To Hell with Fishing* and Bill Naden, President of the Brooklyn Fly-fishers, the oldest club on the upper reaches. Ed and I came out to Doug Bury's Antrim Lodge at Roscoe on the banks of the Willowemoc on the evening of April twelfth, the day before opening. Ed wanted me to see and feel the mood of opening day, and it was there already as fishermen from all over gathered in the bar at the Lodge. Everyone knew everyone. Everyone was relaxed about the prospects of fishing, which were plainly less than good, but stirred by the pleasures of re-union, the sense of taking part in this special occasion that had been shared in the past by so many of the great names of fly-fishing, by so many friends and, often enough, by fathers and grandfathers, uncles and brothers and sons. It was not hard for me, a simple soul from the far west, where I may still find a new trout stream tomorrow, to feel the mood and be impressed by it. We also have our openings, our reunions, our memories of those who fished before us in many of the same places; but we cannot boast a tradition of such power and authority.

Ed and I went out after a while into the clear, cold night to exercise Ed's big Labrador. There was frost on the grass and the roofs, ice on the puddles; a high moon lighted the riffles of the Willowemoc above the highway bridge and the little town was very quiet after the brightness and talk of Doug Bury's bar.

"There won't be any fishing to speak of," Ed told me, echoing the conviction of nearly everyone we had spoken to inside. "But we'll move up and down the river, crack a bottle or two and talk with a lot of old friends."

I believed him and looked forward happily to the prospect. But I couldn't help hoping there might just be one of those sparse winter hatches of pale duns, a big wise fish, relaxed by his winter of security, rising to them, and myself within range.

Bill Naden joined us early the next morning, and we went downstream at first, all the way to the East Branch of the Delaware, where some of the big browns winter over. The air temperature was 38, the water a discouraging 34. From time to time snow flurries whirled across the brown faces of the hills and settled into the valley. Plenty of fishermen were at work, though the stream certainly was not crowded except at a few favorite pools where optimistic fishermen lined both sides only eight or ten feet apart, fly-men and spinners crossing lines in the same hope that I had briefly held the night before—that some leviathan, off his guard, might stir from bottom and make a mistake, or else that a hungry hatchery yearling would accept an easy offering.

A few, very few, fish were being taken, and those mostly around six or eight inches. "This is opening day," Bill reminded me. "It doesn't mean much except that. Half of these fellows won't show up on the stream again all year and most of the others won't bother after they think the hatchery fish are used up. The real fishing here is in the summer and fall. You can always find a few good fish feeding then if you know the river; and there's a chance of something really big occasionally."

"Some of the big ones move back up from the East Branch when the water warms up," Ed said. "You get some nice hatches at times too."

"Don't any big fish hold over up here?"

"Sure," said Bill. "Some do. Shouldn't be surprised if there's one or two up under our dam on the club water now."

Another snow flurry came down on us then and Bill said: "Let's go and take a quick look at the upper reaches, then get back to the club and have some lunch."

Above its junction with the Willowemoc, the Beaverkill is quite small, a mountain stream rather than a valley stream, with steep slopes running up from its banks in most places—most pleasant slopes, covered by deciduous trees and a few conifers, with rhododendrons growing wild in the leaf mold under them. The trees were not yet leafed and the water was low, almost as I imagined it would be in summertime, with great piles of ice pans in places along the banks and the trunks of waterside trees scarred by the tearing of ice in the break-up. I could see it was not altogether a friendly place for fish to winter over. But there were plenty of good pools and since much of the water is privately owned, by clubs or individuals, a good deal of valuable improvement work has been done. We saw few fishermen, but once, where the road passed close to a good pool, a nice trout of about twelve inches rose smoothly—to a snowflake, as nearly as we could judge.

The Brooklyn Club was founded in 1895 and has its headquarters in a tumbledown farmhouse far older than that. One ancient angler was dozing, glass in hand, in a deep chair before a huge fire in a huge fireplace. Ed suggested he must be thawing out after a morning in the stream; Bill considered it more likely he had braved only the depths of his chair and been overcome by them since breakfast. We talked in whispers and took on a little warmth ourselves while sorting out rods and gear to go out after lunch.

There was a flutter of sunshine, quickly lost in gray cloud as we started out. There was no possible doubt it was a wet-fly day and we were content to tie on wet flies—fairly large streamer patterns at that. We fished the Home Pool, the Twin Rocks and one or two other attractive pools or corners without result, then came to the dam in a minor blizzard that completely hid the far bank. Bill told me he had little doubt there would be a big fish or two spending the last days of his winter's rest somewhere in the deep water under the lip of the dam.

I was more than ready to believe him and went out with fine confidence into the smooth glide of water that slid into the little fall over the wall of rocks. The backward fold of current at the foot of the fall sucked the line down nicely and I could imagine the fly hovering and darting enticingly down in the sheltered water near the bottom. Surely some big brown trout would be hungry down there, surely he must know he would feel better with a nice little minnow firmly down in his stomach; after all, the fish had to start feeding sometime and this could be the moment. So I worked very faithfully with the snow on my face and my eyes half closed to it; but it was not the time and we went back to the Clubhouse fishless, to admire the outlines of splendid *Fontinalis* and *Gairdneri* and *Trutta* that decorated the walls. The ancient angler still slept in his chair, the fire still glowed and we needed warmth.

Surely fly-fishers are the most disregarded of men. This river, of all North American rivers, is the shrine of their sport. In this and others in the Catskills the North American fly-fisher began his serious affairs. "For over a hundred years," wrote Theodore Gordon, more than fifty years ago, "the valley of the Beaverkill has been celebrated for its beauty and the river for its trout." To these streams the tradition crossed the Atlantic, to be steadily reinforced and developed by continuing exchanges between fishermen of the old world and the new.

From these streams, and especially from the Beaverkill, the old traditions, reinforced by the new, went out to the rest of the continent to be tried and used and still further adapted until they fitted the needs of each new place. Surely it is time for the Beaverkill to be set aside as the fly-fisherman's shrine forever. It should be left for fly-fishermen, and fly-fishermen only. Some thought should be given to the possibilities of restoration. Is it too warm for the eastern brook trout, too heavily fished, unsuitable in some other way? If so, what chance would there be of counteracting the difficulty and bringing the fish back as Daniel Webster and Frank Forester and so many others knew them?

Failing this, there is more than enough to be said for the brown trout provided he is reasonably abundant and of respectable size, say from ten inches up—and of course reserved for the fly-fisherman so that the craftier individuals have at least an even chance to last out a few seasons and grow to an impressive size.

The river has been tidied up and its banks are now fairly

well-protected from the activities of garbage dumpers and trash throwers, thanks to the writings of Sparse Grey Hackle in the magazine *Sports Illustrated*. But this seems hardly enough. Isn't there room for some great gesture by fly-fishermen all over the United States and Canada to have this one river set aside as a perpetual monument to the sport—a monument that many might never see, but all should know?

After all, it shouldn't be such a tremendous task. The stream still has most of its natural beauty. The valley still has its great fly-tiers and conservationists like the Darbees and the Dettes. It still has its magic name. Above all it still has its faithful few, sons and grandsons and by now even great-grandsons of those who originally fished there, as well as those who have found it more recently. A Derbyshire fisherman wrote me just the other day: "I have recently fished Walton and Cotton's stretch of the Dove. The Fishing Hut and the cut-off tree trunk for lunch outside are still there."

Is it too much to ask, for all of North America, just one stream so dedicated and protected forever?

4. *Blackhole*

Every so often I find myself thinking of a possible return to the streams of my extreme youth, the Dorsetshire Frome and Wrackle, in England. They are not famous or spectacular rivers, but perfect small trout streams, ideal dry-fly streams with a respectable abundance of trout running from ten inches up to two pounds. Anything over a pound is a good fish; anything over a pound and a half is an exceptional fish. But even the smaller ones must be approached with a decent measure of respect and caution and skill if one hopes to do business with them. A catch of half-a-dozen twelve- to fourteen-inch fish is perfectly good reason for a measure of pride—the man who makes it is a competent performer.

It is now nearly thirty years since I have seen or fished either stream, though I was fairly close to them for a short while during the war years. It is perfectly normal to want to go back and see them again and I know I should find them both less and more than my memories of them. What puzzles me is that I think now almost always of Blackhole.

Blackhole is just that, a deep black hole of a pool at a right angle bend in the Wrackle, immediately above a hatchway and a narrow bridge, not ten minutes' walk from my grandfather's, now my cousin's, house. There are always some big fish in Blackhole, fish from one and a half to two pounds, and one goes there hoping to find one of them up

in feeding position. Sometimes a good fish has dropped
back through the hatchway and will be feeding over the
apron below. Here he is likely to be easy and not really like
a Blackhole fish at all—in fact he may very well have come
up from the pool below.

Sometimes there may be one or several good fish rising
nicely at the head of the pool, just where the weed beds
and gravel break off into the depths. If so the best of them
will probably be feeding farthest upstream, with the others
so close that any disturbance from them will put him
down—he is well-protected, but not impossible and there
is always a chance he may be up there alone. Or there may
be a good fish rising nicely against the withy-bed on the far
side; apart from the problem of drag, he should not be too
difficult. Yet another likely possibility is a big fish cruising
in the eddy at the dead end of the pool, past the flow that
leads into the hatches. This is difficult because the end of
the pool has a bank four or five feet high and it is difficult
to get into position to find and cover the fish without being
seen.

Finally, and most difficult of all, there is the fish who
stations himself immediately above the hatch openings. He
cannot be reached from below, because the hatch openings
are too narrow and the banks are too high. From above
he is just possible, but again there is the high bank, the
probability that some movement of rod or man will be seen
and certainty of drag on anything short of a perfect cast.

These are all nice problems, just the sort of things one
should be remembering and hoping to test oneself against
once more. I remember them—in fact I think I have cata-
logued them with very fair accuracy—but these are not

really the things I think of when I remember Blackhole.
I think, instead, of the minnows.

It happened, not infrequently, that one came to Blackhole and found no fish rising, or else that one completely
messed up whatever was rising and put it off the feed for
several days. This is where the minnows came in.

A casual fly, dabbled over the high bank on to the surface
of the eddy, would bring them up. The first time it happened was pure accident. I hooked one through the body
cavity, somewhere around the pectoral fins, and somehow
the tiny hook killed it instantly. I looked it over, then
dropped it back into the water, still on the hook. It sank
instantly and went slowly down, twisting and shining, into
the black velvet depths. I let it go, not altogether without
evil intent, and watched it down through eight or ten feet
until it came to rest, still white and shining, on the dark surface of weed at the bottom. For a few seconds it was still.
Then it moved as though nudged. Then it was carried a
little distance. Then it disappeared altogether. I waited a
moment, struck as hard as I dared and hooked a large,
rather ugly, very dark trout. I landed him and killed him,
not quite sure whether to feel pride or shame.

Once started, I pursued my vice fairly regularly. I would
give the pool an honest try, and then, if nothing came of
it and I was not in a hurry to move on upstream, I would
dabble the fly for a minnow. Very often I didn't hook one.
Very often when I did hook one and let it sink down into
the pool, nothing would bother to take it. Quite often, a
good fish took my minnow, but the little fly hook pulled
free without touching him when I struck. Occasionally I
hooked a big fish and at least once a fine fish, pale and

beautifully marked and in perfect condition. That time I did feel ashamed. But the fascination persisted and evidently it has persisted right to this day. I can't explain it exactly. Partly, I suppose, it was different, a sharp change from every aspect of normal fishing. And it was exciting to watch the minnow stirred by some unseen creature, to watch and wait for its final disappearance. But mostly, I think, the fascination was in not knowing what might be tempted. Blackhole is the sort of place to look for a monster and I think we all believed in our hearts that monsters might be there, fish of three or four pounds, larger than anything we had ever known in that part of the stream. We hoped always to find such a fish, well up in the water and rising steadily where the run came in at the head of the pool. That we did not find him so did not mean he might not be there, somewhere in the depths of the pool, sulkily lurking in wait for just such a morsel as a freshly killed minnow drifting down from above. My minnow experiments may have proved that this was wishful thinking, but nothing like that stays proved. Leviathan might have grown suddenly, between one season and the next. And after thirty seasons, unless some other poacher has been dabbling a dead minnow, who is to say he is not there?

I have more respectable thoughts than this about the streams of my youth, though none so compelling. There is the sharp bend below the pool we called Hatch-hole, on the Frome—many of our best pools were below the hatch-weirs that were used to divert water through carriers and ditches into the meadows. There is a broad rushing shallow below Hatch-hole and the water gathers from this into a swift glide under a cut bank on the bend. Over the cut bank a vicious blackberry bush drops its branches to the surface of the water; against these a drift of foam and little sticks and broken weeds collects. Nearly always there is a good trout rising daintily against the very edge of the drift. He will not move out for a fly and the current along the edge of the drift is a fraction slower than the current farther out, so the cast must not only be accurate, but a little curved to delay drag. I should like to try for him, and to do so quite without any nonsense about minnows or wet flies or even nymphs.

Then there are the brushy, overgrown places that it was custom to pass up. I know a lot more now about brush and trees and I should not pass them up. It would be satisfying to prove that age can achieve where youth did not venture.

I think what I mostly want from the rivers of youth is a fair shot at a rising fish, and by "fair shot" I mean one that gives little or no margin for error. I should like to try them again to see just how difficult they are. In sum those rivers could not offer me what I have found in the western streams—the splendid uncertainty of the migrant runs, the difficulties of fast water, the summer steelhead lying out in the open runs waiting for a dry fly, the rainbows and cut-throats in the lovely runs and pools of the mountain streams. They take more spectacularly, fight much faster and harder and usually they are more beautiful on the beach. But I have an uneasy feeling that too often they are suckers—I hook them not because I have done exactly the right things in exactly the right way, but because I happened to be there with the right gear at the right time.

The Elk River here on the Campbell watershed, for in-stance, gives one many a fair shot at a rising fish. It is a swift gravelly mountain stream, good mainly for cutthroats and a few small rainbows, and a fair shot at a rising fish means, almost certainly, a fish risen and a fish hooked. The fly may drag and he may follow and take it. If he misses, ten to one he will move back into place and offer a second chance.

Two or three years ago my son Alan and I came down to a nice little pool on the upper reaches of the Elk. It was smooth and clear with an easy current through it, a log jam on the far side and a fierce rapid below. The day was hot and bright, but a good fish of fifteen inches was rising over the body of the pool, a little more than halfway up. As I settled on the gravel bar to put a fly over him I saw the shadow of a much larger fish moving under the log jam. For a moment I hesitated. It seemed better to set the fly close against the log jam and give the big fellow a chance to come out at it before disturbing the pool. But when I looked for him again I could not find him, so I set the fly over the smaller fish and hooked him at once.

It was a strong fish and under the bright sun the disturbance in the small pool was formidable, even though I hurried him back to the tail and into the rapid, where Alan did a quick and skillful job of netting. When we came back to the pool, there was the big fish lying out in the middle. There seemed not the slightest doubt that the disturbance had attracted him.

I put the fly over him and he took it at once. For a few seconds he was hooked and struggling, then the fly came away.

"Struck too quickly," I told Alan. "Where did he go? Back under the log jam?"

The ripples were still clearing from the still surface of the pool. "No," Alan said. "I think he's right where he was. Only on the bottom."

I looked and could see him, a big dark shape right down on the bottom in the deepest part of the pool. I began to dry off my fly and let out line.

"Why don't you change your fly?" Alan asked. "Try a wet, maybe?"

"He'd have to be a damn fool to take anything now," I said. "So he may as well have another look at this."

I set the fly up over him twice and at the second drift I thought I saw his pectorals spread and quiver. At the next drift I thought he lifted almost imperceptibly from the bottom. At the sixth or seventh he came up slowly and beautifully, all the way, and took the fly perfectly. I gave him lots of time, then set the hook solidly. He was away for his log jam at once, but I turned him. He came back, then tried for it again until the side pressure swung him away. The next move, I felt sure, would be for the rapid, and so it was. But Alan was waiting at the lip with the net. The fish checked for a foolish moment, I held as hard as 4x gut would stand and Alan had him—eighteen inches long and slightly over two pounds, which is a big fish for the Elk. But I hadn't caught him. He had committed suicide.

Between this fish and the fish that will be rising from under the drift in the bend below Hatch-hole next summer, there is a great gulf of difference. Both give the sharpest kinds of pleasure a trout fisherman can ask for. I would settle happily for either, but it is nice to keep both freshly in mind. What there is about the minnows, I am not quite sure. Perhaps they bridge the gulf between the wild and the sophisticated.

PART EIGHT
Conclusion

1. *What Is Good?*

Fisherman's luck is proverbial, though I am never quite sure whether it is proverbially good or bad. The fisherman's traditional greeting is supposed to be: "Any luck?" though I must say I prefer the more reasonable: "Done any good?" or better still: "Anything moving?" which begs the issue of personal performance. The everlasting question of small boys met by the streamside: "Caught anything?" is just a little too challenging to be comfortable.

Once I worked for some months on a survey crew with a little Irishman who cursed his luck from morning to night. If he made a miscalculation or drove a hub in the wrong place or lost his way or tripped on a root or cut himself with an ax, his invariable exclamation was: "The curse of Cromwell and all the Royal Family on the luck." For anything milder, which was most of the time, he simply said: "Curses on the luck." And he was certainly the hardest-luck guy I ever came across. If anything could possibly go wrong, it seemed to go wrong for him. Finally he suffered severe and recurring attacks of cedar poisoning, which forced him to leave the woods. These he bore with a good deal of fortitude and cheerfulness, rarely cursing his luck. But of all the things I saw happen to him, I felt that these attacks were among the very few that could properly be ascribed to luck, good or bad.

I was in my late teens at the time of this encounter with little Mac and in self-defense I felt I had to develop a counter-philosophy. This was based on the rather arrogant theory, developed from fairly sharp observation of Mac himself, that there is no such thing as luck—every happening, good or bad, simply reflected good or bad judgment and good or bad execution. This theory never sat very well with Mac, comforting as I tried to make it, so I didn't work it too hard with him. But I put it to good use later on.

Within a year or so I found myself trapping, beachcombing, handlogging and conducting various other activities with a group of young fellows. I was the senior by a few months and for this reason I was accorded a measure of leadership, recognized by an impressive title: The General. My duties were to direct the broader aspects of our strategy, to lead or kick the boys out to work in the mornings and to maintain morale. Besides those I have already mentioned, our activities included rounding up errant bush cattle, commercial fishing in season and occasionally guiding sportsmen, so it is not hard to understand that things often went badly and morale tended to drop pretty far down.

When this happened I allowed no one to blame his luck—if he tried it, everyone quickly pointed out errors of judgment or execution that had caused it. And by the same token anyone could claim the fullest possible credit for every triumph he achieved, he could boast and strut as much as he wanted and everyone was bound to agree with him. So long as he had taken full blame for things that went wrong, he was entitled to full credit for things that went right.

The morality of all this and its effect on our developing characters may have been doubtful. But it kept us all surprisingly happy and good-tempered and it seemed to lead to a fair measure of achievement. And under the circumstances, it was a fairly easy philosophy to support. If a man goes out to shoot a buck or trap a mink or catch a fish or float a log off the beach, and brings home his buck, his mink, his fish or his log, plainly he has achieved his purpose and is entitled to say: "I planned it that way." Similarly, if he fails, it is easy enough to think of many little things which, if handled differently, would probably have made the difference between success and failure.

For many years I was content to apply the same theory to my fishing—for anything that went wrong I was prepared to blame myself, for anything that went right I was prepared to take all the credit. Fishing, I argued, was an exact performance, a simple contest between man and fish. If the man judged his conditions right and did the right things, he would catch his fish; if he did not, he would not.

On the whole it works out fairly well, especially so far as the blame is concerned. Such things as the frayed leader, the knot that should have been re-tied, the good lie approached too carelessly, the clumsy cast, the poorly timed strike, the fish held too hard or too lightly, or hurried too much in the final moments, are all errors of judgment or performance which fully justify the disasters they may, and often do not, produce. Only rarely do I miss or lose a fish when I feel I have done everything right, and only once have I broken in a fish when I felt it was in no smallest way my fault. That fish was the biggest brown trout I hooked in South America, a veritable monster of well over ten pounds who had fought his fight and was permitting himself to be led quietly to the beach when the break came. It was not the line, nor the leader, nor even the rod that broke, but the hook, suddenly and, so far as I am concerned, unaccountably to this day.

On the credit side, I am beginning to have rather more trouble with my fine theory. True, there are plenty of times when one makes a plan, follows it through and everything works out exactly as it should. One has no difficulty in taking credit for these occasions.

But I am beginning to find it very salutary to remember just how much "happening right," if not downright luck, there has been in nearly all my little triumphs. Often there has been so little between success and failure that I feel little inclined to take much credit unless for perseverance, and that is no virtue because I do not persevere in fishing unless I am enjoying myself. Time and again one or two fish, seldom more than half-a-dozen, make the day. How close a thing has it been between getting or not getting those few fish?

I think of big fish that have taken a dragging fly, or an accidentally drowned fly or of clumsy casts that should have put them down. They look just as well in the fisherman's triumphant return as the fish that took on the perfect drift from the perfect cast. How often has the one good fish of the day dropped the fly from his mouth as the net lifted him—and I am never reluctant about giving a fish slack, believing as I do that if he is properly hooked no amount of slack will shake the barb. I have landed rushing summer steelhead that were hooked only by a shred of skin in the point of the jaw and taken full credit for them; no doubt I have lost far more of these than I have landed, but a fish that is properly deceived and accurately tightened on is not hooked by a sliver of skin in the point of the jaw. How often has the fish that made the day come from a place that one cast to, not with conviction, but in desperation?

All these things are quite special pleasures and, in their way, special triumphs. They are the heart and soul of fishing, the unexpected, the unpredictable, the unorthodox, the quite simple and natural yield of dealing with a wild creature rather than an inanimate thing. There cannot be too many of them for me and I am only too happy to enjoy them to the full. I only wonder a little about the ethics of taking credit for them or, more difficult to control, being given credit for them. And this in turn makes me wonder just who and what is a "good fisherman" or a "skillful fisherman." I sometimes suspect he may be one like me who fishes often enough and hard enough to get the breaks.

I can think of few angling undertakings more unlikely than that of catching a winter steelhead to order on the fly. The first time I ventured on this I openly and vaingloriously boasted that I would take a fish from a small pool where spinner-fishermen had just previously hooked nine fish and, so they thought, exhausted the possibilities. I worked a fly down carefully through half-a-dozen casts to the best lie in the pool and had my fish. It was an admirable proceeding in every way except that I was rather more surprised by the result than were those who watched.

My second venture of this sort was an unconscious one. I went up the river with a well-known outdoor writer and his wife who said they would like to catch a fish on the fly. They suggested I demonstrate, which I did by hooking a fish, again in a very favorable lie, within a few minutes. My friend the writer then said: "I was sure glad to see you do that. I know you have written about it a lot, but a good many people say it's all nonsense, it can't be done." The people he quoted weren't really so far off the mark, at that. Unless you have a good lie and a fish happens to be in it, it can be quite difficult to take a winter fish on the fly. This, of course, looked easy. And later in the afternoon I was able to hang my fly in the quieter water where two fast runs angled together and pick up another fish. So it looked both easy and consistent. Yet how many times I have fished those same places, just as well and just as carefully, in vain.

Once I caught a winter fish for a photographer, himself a keen summer fly-fisherman, in the Line Fence Pool, just above my house. I even told him where I would be standing when the fish took, if he took. And it was so; within half an hour we were back at the house with photographs and a twelve-pounder. "When I saw you go out with that thing," said the photographer, pointing to the fly, "I thought you were kidding. I didn't think they would take a fly." *

Less than a year later I tried to do the same thing for my friend Dunc Marshall. I fished through the same lie and another good one without a touch. Because the river was a bit high I kept going, swung the fly in behind a rock where I had never hooked a fish before, and was taken solidly. So also with my friend Tony Bristowe, a most sophisticated fisherman. Things had been very bad on the Campbell for at least two weeks—there simply were no fish, for the fly or anything else. "Come on out, anyway," Tony said. "I want to see how you fish for them." We went to another favorite place and again fished through the good lies without a touch. There was water below where I had caught occasional summer fish, but never a winter fish though I had worked it often. This day there was a fish in it and he took the fly and it all looked very impressive, even to Tony who should know better.

---

* Since writing these vainglorious words I have had a further experience of trying to catch winter steelhead for the camera. It worked out disastrously. I shall tell of it, with due humility I hope, when time has mellowed the memory.

Going back to those youthful days I have described, all these would have been sound occasions for claiming credit in no uncertain voice. Now I wonder about them. They sound well in the telling, but they hung by such slender threads of probability that luck seems to hold a far greater share in them than judgment or skill. Too often one has fished at least as thoroughly, under as good or better conditions in the very same places, and had nothing at all to show for it. After all, a good deal depends on the fish—first he must be there and then he must be in the mood to give way to temptation.

I remember many days when I have gone out fishing with two or three pools in mind that I felt certain would give me good results. Sometimes the expected happens; the fish are where past experience says they should be, feeding as they should be and all is well. But surprisingly often it doesn't work out that way at all. The favorite pools produce little or nothing, while lesser pools make the day. Something is wrong with experience or with the fisherman's interpretation of experience. Again a touch of humility seems in order, though one can scarcely be expected to remember it. More probably one takes credit for intelligent opportunism in finding new places.

At this stage I find myself wondering just what it was I had in mind when I asked myself the question at the head of this chapter. Was I wondering what makes a fisherman good, or what makes fishing good? I am pretty sure it must have been the second of these, because I seem to remember having decided elsewhere that a good fisherman is simply one who gets really keen and lively pleasure from his fishing. And this to some extent explains the confusion, because the two things rather plainly go together.

To Frederick Halford, good fishing was the taking of wise, feeding brown trout on a surface fly that matched the natural and so brought triumph through complete deception. Skues was willing to try below the surface as well as on it, though in much the same terms, and certainly made a lot of additional pleasure for himself and others in so doing. La Branche, working under different conditions, was willing to search for trout in likely places and, if necessary, persuade them by persistent and accurate casting that a natural hatch had come on the water. Wood of Cairnton liked to take his salmon on a single-handed rod with a small fly fished right up in the surface film. When he did everything right he moved fish that would move for nothing else and usually hooked them securely in the corner of the mouth—a fine performance calling for great skill and control, and no doubt yielding a lively sense of pleasure and triumph.

But these and other good men, I am sure, have less precise tests which make them say: This was a good day's fishing; that was a poor one. Such a comment might or might not bear a close relationship to the fisherman's estimate of his own performance—it is not likely to be altogether independent of it, for few of us are objective enough to recognize a day in which everything we did was wrong as a good day. But it will certainly be compounded of many things beyond our control—the weather, the performance of the fish, perhaps other happenings along the stream only tenuously connected with the fishing itself.

Every fisherman worthy of the name sets certain conditions upon his sport. The more skillful and the more experienced he is, the more exacting these are likely to be and the greater his pleasures when he fulfills them all and still comes home from the river with a good catch. Within his chosen conditions, he is always hoping and striving for this desirable result. But if it ever came about that he could achieve the result with anything approaching mechanical certainty, he would have lost his sport. He would be having uninteresting days—bad ones rather than good. The only thing to do then would be to set himself some new conditions, or else give up fishing. From time to time in a fisherman's life, it does turn out that he has to set himself new conditions. Usually this is because he has found some new and more exacting or more exciting way of engaging the attentions of his fish rather than because the results of the old one have become too certain. The new conditions or the new method open up a whole new field of exploration and the days are once more lively and good. But I think it is altogether possible that we might in the end wear out all the possible combinations of conditions and methods were it not for one thing—the unpredictability of the fish.

So long as water moves, so long as fins press against it, so long as weather changes and man is fallible, fish will remain in some measure unpredictable. And so long as there is unpredictability, there will be luck, both good and bad.

I don't wish for bad luck. I think I can honestly say I prefer a difficult undertaking skillfully carried through to a successful ending above any amount of good luck. But I am inclined to admit at this late date that there is always a certain amount of luck in fishing. One can do something to reduce the chances of either kind, but that is all. And it is just as well. So long as there are fish in the wrong places, taking in the wrong way, at the wrong times, fishing will never be dull. And so long as one shouts occasionally into the laughing waters a good, heartfelt "Damn the luck!" fishing will remain an exciting and enthralling sport. It is perfectly true that good fishing is not all luck. But it is just as true that there is no good fishing without some luck.